YOU AND YOUR DIABETES

By the same author :

- जीवन मधुमेह के संग
- हृदय रोग और आपः रोग, उपचार एवं सावधानियाँ
- डायबिटीज प्रश्नोत्तरी
- Diet And Diabetes
- You And Your Diabetes
- Diabetes Quiz Book

About the Author

Dr. Ashok K. Jhingan, (*b.* 1949) M.B.B.S., M.D. Medicine, has worked as Senior Consultant in Medicine, Deptt. in Jaipur Golden Hospital and National Heart Institute and is a visiting Consultant in Sir Ganga Ram Hospital, Delhi. At present he is also a consultant Diabetologist with BHEL.

Author started working in the field of Diabetes since 1983 and has organised Diabetes Detection and Education Camps in and around Delhi.

Author is a firm believer of the fact that Diabetic who know most, lives longest.

Author has written six books on diabetes and heart problems (in Hindi and English). These books have been appreciated by masses and this is evident from the fact that their new editions had to be brought out.

Delhi Diabetes Research Centre (DDRC) is a registered society and was established by group of doctors from India and abroad along with diabetes Educators and Nutrition Experts. Its sole aim is to help and educate Diabetics by arranging regular seminars and conferences, so that they can lead normal life with diabetes. So far we have organised 130 such camps in and around Delhi. Every year we organize 3 day Diabetes Health Melas which is being attended by thousands of people. These melas have created diabetes awareness in masses.

Dr. Ram Mohan Jhingan, M.D., is doing his fellowship in endocrinology from Temple University, Philadelphia. U.S.A. He is associated with Delhi Diabetes Research Centre and is actively involved with the educational and awareness activities of this Centre.

4th Revised & Enlarged Edition

You and Your Diabetes

Dr. Ashok K. Jhingan
M.B.B.S., M.D. (Medicine), FIAMS
Chairman
Delhi Diabetes Research Centre (DDRC)
&
Dr. Ram Mohan Jhingan M.D.

CONCEPT PUBLISHING COMPANY PVT. LTD.,
NEW DELHI-110059

ISBN-13 : 978-81-8069-879-8

4th Revised & Enlarged Edition 2012

Published and Printed by

Concept Since 1974

Concept Publishing Company Pvt. Ltd.
A/15-16, Commercial Block, Mohan Garden
New Delhi-110059 (India)
T: 25351460, 25351794, *F*: 091-11-25357109
E: publishing@conceptpub.com, W: www.conceptpub.com
Editorial Office: H-13, Bali Nagar, New Delhi-110 015, India.

Cataloging in Publication Data--*Courtesy:* D.K. Agencies (P) Ltd. <docinfo@dkagencies.com>

Jhiṅgana, E. Ke. (Aśoka Ke.), 1949-
You and your diabetes / Ashok K. Jhingan & Ram Mohan Jhingan. — 4th rev. & en.ed.
p. cm.
ISBN 9788180698798

1. Diabetes—Popular works. 2. Diabetes—Prevention. I. Jhingan, Ram Mohan, joint author. II. Title.

DDC 616.462 23

This book is
Dedicated
To
All the Scientists, Doctors, Nurses, Social Workers and Individuals who are Engaged in the Welfare of Diabetic Patients

Do You Know?

- Diabetes is the fifth largest killer disease
- People with Diabetes have more problems like
  —Heart Attack
  —Paralytic Strokes
  —Blindness
  —Kidney Failure
  —Sexual Problems
  —Frequent Infections.
- Majority of Diabetics think it is not a major health problem.
- 80 per cent Diabetic Patients are Unaware of the Complications of Diabetes.

Foreword

A person with Diabetes requires full information regarding various do's and don'ts in everyday living.

It is very essential that Diabetics realize their own responsibilities in control of Blood Glucose and the requirement of medications.

A person with Diabetes has to be aware of certain emergencies and in such events how these may be circumvented.

Dr. A.K. Jhingan has fulfilled the needful requirement of Diabetes in our country. In a very simple language and practical manner, view points of a Diabetologist are presented.

I sincerely hope that full use of this information is made by Diabetics.

Late **Dr. M.M.S. Ahuja**
Formerly Prof. and Head
Department of Endocrinology and
Metabolic Unit,
A.I.I.M.S.

Preface to the Fourth Edition

First edition of the book "You and Your Diabetes" was published in 1988. Since then we are witnessing a global epidemic of diabetes and obesity. So prevention and treatment will require an in-depth understanding of the therapeutic options. It is therefore timely and appropriate that this book has been dedicated to the topic of various therapeutic strategies in diabetes and its various complications.

In the first part, Diet and Nutrition, we have tried to give detailed information about the diet and disadvantages of overcooking. As a variety of blood glucose lowering drugs are now available with different mode of actions and their safety profiles are discussed in details.

Effect of long-term diabetes on Gastrointestinal tract, urinary system and oral problems in Diabetes are added in this edition. Use of Insulin Pumps as a better mode of administration of insulin and for good control of diabetes has been added. New topics like Diabetes and Menopause and about Obesity are also discussed in this enlarged and revised edition.

We hope that you will enjoy reading these new chapters, as we have, and that you will find them useful.

Dr. Ashok K. Jhingan

25 November, 2011 **Dr. Ram Mohan Jhingan**

Preface to the Second Edition

You and your Diabetes was published in 1998. The message of the new edition of this book is that Medical science moves forward and most of the questions stay the same but many of the answers have changed. The outlook for people with diabetes improves year by year.

One thing remains unchanged, the absolute necessity for people with diabetes to learn and understand as much as they can about their disease. Ignorance is often damaging and can sometimes be lethal. More information is available about prevention of prime factors which produce complications of Diabetes and new treatment modalities like islet cell transplantation, pancreas cell transplantation, new ways of Insulin delivery system, i.e., pens and pumps and new group of oral medicines which reduce Insulin resistance and help in controlling blood sugar levels.

People with diabetes will also want to keep themselves updated and well-informed and we hope this new edition will be of help to them.

Dr. Kamalesh Jhingan

Introduction

So many books about diabetes have been written and the reader gets more confused going through lengthy chapters about the disease. After discussing with many patients of Diabetes it was felt that there should be a book in simple language which should be informative as well as interesting.

Diabetes is a disease which can be very well controlled and one can lead a normal life. Complications of Diabetes can make the life of Diabetic miserable due to Blindness, Kidney failure, Neuritis and Paralysis.

Recently a study was conducted in insulin dependent Diabetic patients and according to it, if these patients keep their blood sugar under control then blindness can be prevented in the 76 per cent of such patients, kidney failure in 35 to 56 per cent of such Diabetic patients and Neuritis (Nerve involvement) in 60 per cent of such Diabetic patients.

Intensive control of Diabetes Mellitus decreases the rate of complications, improves the patients quality of life, and decreases the total cost of care associated with both type I and type II Diabetes. Study, the United Kingdom Prospective Diabetes Study (UKPDS) of 1998, have confirmed that the Goal in type II Diabetes must also be normalization or near normalization of the blood glucose level in order to decrease associated complications.

Idea of writing this book is to give information to all Diabetic patients about the disease and its complications in a simple language so that they can understand these and can lead normal life.

Dr. Ashok K. Jhingan
Chairman
Delhi Diabetic Research Centre

J-136, Rajouri Garden,
New Delhi
Phones : 25419776, 25419777
25163623, 25163624

Acknowledgements

More than 40,000 Diabetic patients who are registered with DDRC and attend this clinic regularly and provide information which is utilized in the interest of developing newer and better modes of treatment.

Experiences of many Physicians and Diabetic Educators has helped me to prepare this book.

I would like to thank the Management of DDRC, who have helped me in great extent in preparing 3rd edition of this book.

I am also thankful to the Management and Staff of State Bank of India, who have helped me in organizing the Diabetes detection and education camps.

Pharmaceutical companies like NOVO-NORDISK (INDIA) PVT. LIMITED, BOEHRINGER MANNHEIM, HOECHST, ELI LILLY, RANBAXY LIMITED, SERDIA AND B.D. have also helped in providing educational materials in organising Diabetes detection and education camps.

My wife Dr. Kamalesh and children Dr. Kavita and Dr. Ram Mohan need special mention as without their cooperation this book would not have been completed.

In the end my special thanks to member and staff of Concept Publishing Company Pvt. Ltd. who helped me to accomplish the task of completing this 3rd edition of this book.

Dr. Ashok K. Jhingan

Contents

*Foreword by **Prof. M.M.S. Ahuja*** vii
Preface to the Fourth Edition ix
Preface to the Second Edition x
Introduction xi
Acknowledgements xii

- Diabetes Mellitus 1
- Symptoms of Diabetes 6
- Testing of Sugar 8
- Treatment of Diabetes Mellitus 15
- Diabetes and High Blood Pressure 72
- Disadvantages of Over Cooking 75
- Lifestyle 79
- Exercise 80
- Role of Yoga 86
- Drug Treatment 89
- Insulin 96
- Insulin Pumps 103
- Spontaneous Hypoglycaemia 105
- Diabetic Coma (Hyperglycaemia) 109
- Diabetes Ketoacidosis in Children 112
- Obesity or Over Weight 117
- Diabetes and Heart Problems 120
- Diabetes and Pregnancy 123
- Diabetes and Eyes 127
- Diabetes and Menopause 133
- Dental Care in Diabetes 134
- Nerve Involvement in Diabetes 138
- Skin and Sexual Problems in Diabetes 140
- Diabetes and Kidney Problems 149
- The Digestive System and Urinary Tract System 153

- Emergency in Diabetes 157
- Diabetes in Old Age 158
- Diabetes in Children 160
- Monitoring of Diabetes 168
- Views of Diabetic Patients About their Disease 171
- Alcohol and Diabetes 172
- Diabetes and Smoking 175
- Vacations, Travel and Diabetes 178
- Are You Losing Weight 181
- Diabetes Prevention and High Risk Group to Develop Diabetes 182
- Diabetes and Depression 183
- Aspirin for Diabetics 184
- Are You in High Risk Group for Diabetes 186
- My Story of Diabetes 187
- Foot Care in Diabetes 190
- HbA_{1C} & Mean Blood Glucose 193
- Self-Evaluation About Diabetes Control 198
- Questions Diabetic Patient Usually Ask 200
- Important Points to Remember 202
- Diabetes Care During Other Infections 203
- Stress and Diabetes 205
- Diet During Illness 207
- Foods Can be Used Freely 208
- Diet Charts 210
- Calories Values 224

Diabetes Mellitus

Diabetes Mellitus is a word derived from Greek word Diabetos which means Siphon, Mellitus means Sweet, i.e. "flowing of sweet liquid."

There is mention of this disease by Ayurvedic physician Susruta in Ayurveda in about 400 B.C. and he had described it as "Honeyed urine." Charak, another physician of that time was also well aware of this disease.

At present there are about 157 million people in the world with diabetes and many more may not be aware of their problem. It is expected that by the year 2025 this number would be around 300 million. Many more may not be aware about this disease and they may come to know only while undergoing tests for some problem or when they develop some complication of this disease.

What is Diabetes?

Main items of food are carbohydrates, proteins, fats, vitamins, minerals and water. Whatever food we take, from stomach it goes to small intestine then to large intestine. Many enzymes which come from stomach, gall bladder, liver, small intestine and pancreas gland, mix with food to make it more digestible. Carbohydrates are converted into glucose which gets into the blood stream and ultimately to cells of body to provide energy. This process of absorption of glucose from intestines and to enter into the cells of body is regulated through the "hormone" called Insulin, secreted by gland called 'Pancreas'. In the deficiency of this hormone (Insulin), glucose will not enter into the cells and would remain in blood stream. Thus Blood Sugar will remain high and this sugar will pass in urine. As cells do not get sugar, there will be no energy. Person would feel weak and this will result in weight loss.

Normal Blood Sugar Level

Normal fasting Blood Sugar should be between 70 mgm to 100 mgm per 100ml of Blood. Blood Sugar 2 hours after food should be less than 140mg/ 100ml of Blood. When Blood Sugar is above this level, it means person is suffering from Diabetes.

When the Blood Sugar is persistently high it circulates through kidney and other organs of body, as it is not entering the cells. Kidney cannot cope with this increased level of glucose and glucose escapes into the urine. Glucose will not appear in the urine until and unless Blood Sugar is above 180mg/100ml of Blood.

When there is absolute deficiency of Insulin, fats also escape from fat cells and this fat is converted into Ketones, an acidic substance, by then more and more Ketones are released by liver into blood circulation it leads to *Ketoacidosis*. Ketones appear in urine. Ketones are not present in urine of a normal person.

So now you know that Insulin Hormone is very essential for the entry of glucose into cells and in the absence of this Hormone Blood Sugar level rises, sugar appear in urine and in the severe deficiency of this Hormone, ketones also appear in urine which is a dangerous stage.

Insulin is secreted from Beta Cells of Pancrease gland located in the abdomen. How and why it stops functioning it is not known.

There are many factors which may be responsible for this stage which are discussed below.

Heredity

You must have observed that this disease runs in family. Many members of one family are suffering from diabetes. From parents, through genes, it is transmitted to children, children will have defect in the Beta Cells which produce Insulin and so they become prone to develop diabetes.

This is commonly seen in Type II diabetes as compared to Type I diabetes.

Chances of Developing Diabetes

There are 25 to 30 per cent chances of developing diabetes in the children of Type II diabetic patients.

If one parent is Type II Diabetic—Chances are 27%

If both parent are Type II Diabetic—Chances are 49%

(HLA Antigens are associated with type I diabetes)

Viruses. There are some studies which say that children who suffered from various virus diseases in childhood develop diabetes.

Obseity (Motapa). Obesity certainly predispose the individual to Diabetes specially Type II.

It is said that if person is 30 to 40 per cent over weight than the weight indicated in standard height and weight tables, efficacy of Insulin is decreased by 30 to 40 per cent.

There is insulin resistance. Although these patients are having high levels of insulin in the blood yet their Blood Sugar levels are high.

Diet

It has been observed that people who eat more refined sugars and diet rich in carbohydrate are prone to develop Diabetes. Incidence of Diabetes is higher in Indians who have migrated to U.K. or USA than the local inhabitants. The reason is that they might be having genetic predisposition and by consuming more sugar and carbohydrates in diet, they become obese, which itself is a risk factor for developing diabètes.

Diet rich in fibre reduces the incidence of Diabetes.

Drugs

Many drugs predispose Diabetes. Drugs like steroids used for Allergy and Asthma problems can aggravate diabetes.

Diuretics

Drugs which increase urine flow are used for high Blood pressure can also aggravate diabetes. These drugs lower Postassium which interfere with Insulin release thereby causing high Blood Sugar.

Oral contraceptives also increase Blood Sugar levels.

Lifestyle

Persons who are having borderline diabetes i.e. Diabetes is yet not diagnosed but when exposed to stress in life, will manifest as a full-fledged disease. Sometimes, when you are undergoing investigation for some other disease like Chronic Diarrhoea, longstanding infection or extreme weakness, tests will reveal that you are having high Blood Sugar levels.

Types of Diabetes Mellitus

Types of Diabetes depends upon the status of Insulin Hormone in the body. They are Type I or Type II.

A. Type I or IDDM

If there is no Insulin or very less amount of Insulin then one has to be given Insulin injections regularly and this is called as 'Insulin Dependent Diabetes Mellitus' or IDDM or Type I Diabetes. These patients are young with rapid onset. If Insulin injections are not given to them, they develop ketones in urine and develop *Ketoacidosis* and *coma*. They can lead a normal life with regular injections of Insulin. It usually manifests at a younger age group (4-5 yrs.) and these children would require daily Injections of Insulin to survive.

B. Type II DM or NIDDM

In these patients either there is deficiency of Insulin or resistance to the normal insulin action in the body. Usually there is family history of Diabetes in these patients. This is again of two types:

(a) Obese NIDDM — those who are over weight
(b) Non-Obese NIDDM

More than 2/3rd of all Diabetic patients are suffering from Type II Diabetes. In this group of patients Diabetes can be controlled by Diet Restriction, Regular Exercise, and Oral Hypoglycaemic Agents, i.e. Tablets. Insulin injections are usually not required, initially, but later they may also require Insulin injections.

Symptoms of Diabetes

One of the most important symptoms of Diabetes is:
* Extreme weakness or lethargy.

Common Symptoms of Diabetes

Excessive Hunger

Excessive Thirst

Excessive Urination

Loss of Weight

Tiredness

Irritability

Other symptoms are:

* Excessive Appetite.
* Excessive thirst (desire to take more and more water).
* Excessive urination.
* Loss of weight.
* Itching all over body and itching around private parts. Excessive itching around glans and penis in males and around vagina in females.
* Deterioration in vision with frequent changing of glasses.
* Leg cramps—Pain in legs.
* Burning, in both feet and numbness.
* Delayed healing of wound or some infection in the body.

Problems which Diabetics Encounter more often than General Public

* Heart Attacks (Specially at a younger age)
* Strokes, Paralytic Attacks
* Gangrene of Foot—Leading to Amputation of Foot or Toe
* Repeated Attacks of Infections or Boils
* Rapid Deterioration of Vision and Blindness
* Sexual Problems
* Kidney Disease and Need for dialysis or Renal Transplant.
* Giddiness.
* Eyes-blurring of vision or double vision called Diplopia are common eye symptoms in diabetic patients.

There had been increase in the number of Diabetic patients. Reasons behind this increase are:

* Change in lifestyle.
* Change in food habits.
* Awareness about the disease and symptoms. Patients come forward for blood tests and other investigations for the diagnosis of Diabetes.

Testing of Sugar

Various Diabetes detection and education programmes have changed the thinking of general population. Now they believe that early diagnosis of Diabetes and its control can make their life comfortable, free from the complications of Diabetes. There are various methods to diagnose Diabetes. These are:

* Urine Examination for sugar.
* Blood test for glucose.

Urine Examination

Urine can be tested for glucose at home or in laboratory by stick method or by Benedicts test.

Test by Glucostrips

This is simple procedure. There is a chemical at the end of a strip which when comes in contact with urine sugar/glucose changes its colour. One can read and compare the colours with the colours displayed at strip bottle.

How to do it

1. Collect urine in small container and dip the strip in it for a few seconds or one can dip the strip in stream while passing urine.
2. Shake and clean the strip to remove the excess amount of urine on it.
3. After one minute compare the colour of strip with the colours depicted at bottle.

Results

From the strip it will become clear whether one is having sugar or not. +, ++, ++++ of sugar or 0.5 per cent, 1 per cent, 1.5 per cent or 2 per cent.

Depending upon the colour of strip from

* Blue
* Dark Green
* Yellow-Green
* Brown
* Orange.

It is not essential that all Diabetic patients will pass sugar in urine. If Blood Sugar is not more than 180 mg per 100 ml of Blood, Sugar will not appear in urine.

Excessive intake of Vitamin-C or Asprin or Aldomet tablets can give false positive results, i.e. if person is taking the above medicines his urine may not reveal correct picture.

With Benedict Test

This test was a routine test few decades back and is still being done in remote places. Urine is heated with Benedict's solution and change in colour is observed. Depending upon the colour of mixture—If it is Blue, Dark Green, Yellow Green, Orange.

Urine testing for sugar can be done 3-4 times a day in a patient who is using insulin to monitor the dose of Insulin.

Strips for testing Ketone are also available. Urine of Type-I patients should be tested for Ketones.

Blood Sugar Estimation

For Blood Sugar estimation, now-a-days, there are computerised equipment available which can give the results within few minutes. Blood Sugar estimation is done—

A. Fasting Blood Sugar
B. Post Prandial
C. Random

Fasting Blood Sugar is usually between

* 70 mgm—100 mgm/100 ml
* Post Prandial (PP) means two hours after the meals, i.e. food, not two hours after 1st Blood samples were collected. This Blood Sugar should be below 140 mg per cent.

Random Blood Sugar means blood sugar levels at any time of the day which should be below 160mg per cent in normal person.

Blood Sugar can be done by Gluconometer. It is an easy process requires only a drop of blood and you can know the results immediately.

Blood Sugar (Self Analysis—How Much Under Control)

	Empty Stomach (Fasting)	After 2 hours, of Food (PP)
Normal Level	100 mg per cent	140mg per cent
Satisfactory Level	120mg per cent	160mg per cent
Uncontrolled	Above 140mg per cent	Above 200mg per cent

There are many types of Glucometers available in the market at present and are very easy to use.

The strips have pad at one end which reacts with blood and changes its colour which can be read by naked eye or by feeding strip into the Gluconometer which reveals Blood Sugar level.

Method

1. Clean the finger and then press the Autoclix or prick the finger with needle.
2. Massage the finger to bring big drop of blood on yellow pad, i.e. coloured portion of strip.
3. Keep this strip for one minute on a plane surface after drop of blood.
4. Take cotton and clean the blood from the strip in a one process. Don't rub the strip again and again. At this stage you have two options, if you have gluconometer then insert the strip (coloured portion) facing you or you wait for one more minute; if you don't have gluconometer and compare the colours with the colours which are given on bottle. You can read 200mg, 400mg or 500mg per cent or gluconometer will show the Blood glucose level on meter.

Blood Sugar Estimation from Laboratory

You can get the Blood Sugar testing done from a laboratory. Regular Blood Sugar testing is essential to know the result of treatment and one can adjust the dose of Insulin as well as the medicines.

Blood Sugar test should be done twice, i.e. in fasting stage and 2 hours after food.

There is doubt in the mind of all diabetics that the blood sugar estimation by gluconometer is not reliable. It is not true, throughout the world these gluconometers are used. Usually there is difference of 10 to 15 mg in the reading of the gluconometer and the readings from laboratory.

If there is doubt then one can undergo Glucose Tolerance Test.

Glucose Tolerance Test (G.T.T.)

In this test the person is given 75gm of glucose on the day of test and Blood samples are collected every 30 minutes for 2 hours.

Now-a-days the blood samples are taken 0 hour, 1 hour and at 2 hours. Blood glucose more than 180 mgm after 2 hours glucose ingestion is diagnostic of Diabetes.

Precautions

The person who is undergoing G.T.T., should eat normal diet and should exercise regularly and should not be suffering from any serious disease.

1. Person should not eat anything 8 to 10 hours before test.
2. Person undergoing G.T.T., after giving Ist or IInd blood sample should not go for walking otherwise it will alter Blood Sugar levels.
3. He should not smoke during this period.

People who should undergo this test

1. Suspected cases of Diabetes.
2. Persons having Family History of Diabetes.
3. Obese person.
4. Persons suffering from tuberculosis or non-healing ulcers.
5. Family History of heart attacks in young age.
6. Persons whose Blood Sugar level rises during stress phases should undergo this test.

Glycosylated Haemoglobin—HbA1c

Blood test which indicates Blood Sugar levels in a Diabetic patients over a period of last 2-3 months. Specially useful in Diabetes with pregnancy and it helps to give an idea about the efficacy of treatment. If one can afford, one should undergo this test atleast once or twice in a year.

Normal levels are expressed in %. Normal levels are less than 6.4%. If it is persistently above 9% it indicates abnormally high Blood Sugar and need proper control.

Normal	—	4-6%
Pre-Diabetic	—	5.7-6.4%
Diabetic	—	6.5% or more

Reduction of HbA1c below 7% reduces incidence of complication. If the HbA1c levels are kept below or around 6.5% there are less chances of complications.

Summary About Tests for Diabetes

* One should regularly get the urine tested for sugar and keep records.
* If there is history of vomiting and loose motions, get urine tested for Ketones because timely examination of Ketones in urine can prevent the person going into coma.
* At least once in a year urine should be tested for microalbumin. Appearance of Albumin in urine indicates involvement of kidneys in diabetes and at this stage if Blood Sugar is kept under control, further damage to Kidneys can be prevented.
* Each diabetic patient should have blood sugar testing daily if he is on Insulin and once weekly, if he is on tablets.

Self Monitoring

All Diabetics should learn to monitor their diabetes themselves by doing urine test and Blood glucose estimation. This is called as Home Blood Glucose Monitoring (HBGM). You can make diary and can write about Blood Sugar Levels which will indicate that your Diabetes is under control or not. H.B.G.M. is useful in following situations:

1. This is very important for Diabetic patients who are taking Insulin injections. By measuring Blood Sugar they can reduce or increase the Insulin dose and can prevent Hyper or Hypoglycemia.

2. Useful in those patients who are advised strict Diabetes control.
3. In Brittle Diabetics, it is useful where Blood Sugar level fluctuates.
4. In Diabetic patients with kidney involvement.
5. Persons using Insulin pumps or 3-4 injections of Insulin daily.
6. It is very useful in patients of Diabetes with pregnancy.

What is Meant by Good Control

1. Normal blood sugar levels.
2. Weight — as near to ideal as possible.
3. Blood pressure should be normal.
4. Blood cholesterol and triglycerides within normal limits.
5. Glycosylated haemoglobin within normal limits.

Points to Remember

- Capillary Blood from Finger. Values are about 15 mg higher than venous blood i.e. (Blood Tests done in lab)
- Some people may have *High Fasting Blood Sugar* due to high sugar output from liver overnight. But post prandial sugar is normal due to normal insulin response to food.
- Some people have normal fasting sugar due to overnight suppression of hepatic glucose output but have high post prandial sugar high due to poor food stimulated insulin secretions.

Treatment of Diabetes Mellitus

Diabetics who know more about the disease, its complications and how to cope with it can live longer than those who are unaware about it.

Diabetes is a disease which can be controlled by Diet, exercise, oral medications and Insulin. There is no short-cut as regard management of diabetes is concerned. Treatment plan has to be discussed with patient. He has to be informed about side effects of medicines and about complications of Diabetes which will develop if untreated. It requires patience by both patient as well as his or her relatives. Chances of complications can be significantly reduced if Blood Sugar is kept under control.

Food and Nutrition

Good health is a state of complete physical, mental and social well-being and not merely the absence of disease. According to World Health Organization, good health is not just an absence of disease or illness but it involves physical, psychological and social well-being of an individual.

The 3 main components of a healthy lifestyle are:

1. Regular exercise—Exercise can be defined as physical activity that is a planned, structured movement of the body designed to enhance physical fitness.
2. Balanced diet—Eating healthy is also an important component of a healthy lifestyle. (*to be discussed separately*).
3. Stress management—The definition of stress management then, is basically that it is the emotional and physical strian that is caused by our response to pressures from the outside world. This strain varies in terms of

severity and impact from person to person, as each person handles stress differently and responds differently to separate stressors as well, stressors being the factors in our lives that cause us the stress.

Stress is the body's way of responding to any kind of demand, both by good and bad experiences. When people feel stressed by something that is going on around them, their bodies end up reacting to this by releasing chemicals into the blood, and these chemicals give people more energy and strength, but can also have a turnaround effect and end up making them sad or depressed.

Regardless of how severe your stress is or how long you have been dealing with it, for if you notice any symptoms that are a result of this stress, it is very important that you get yourself into see your doctor as soon as you possibly can. Your physician can help you to define your particular stresses and prescribe medications and therapies that can help you on your info on stress management.

Nutrition: The science of foods, nutrients and other substances therein, their action, interaction and balance in relation to health and disease.

Eating well is vital for a healthy and active life. When the nutritional requirements of an individual are not met, it may lead to a condition known as *Malnutrition.*

Malnutrition is a broad term commonly used as an alternative to undernutrition but technically it also refers to overnutrition.

People are malnourished if their diet does not provide adequate calories and protein for growth and maintenance or they are unable to fully utilize the food they eat due to illness (undernutrition).

They are also malnourished if they consume too many calories (overnutrition).

How to overcome Malnutrition

- Balanced diet

— small and frequent meals

— eat or drink nutritional supplement

Development of Undernutrition

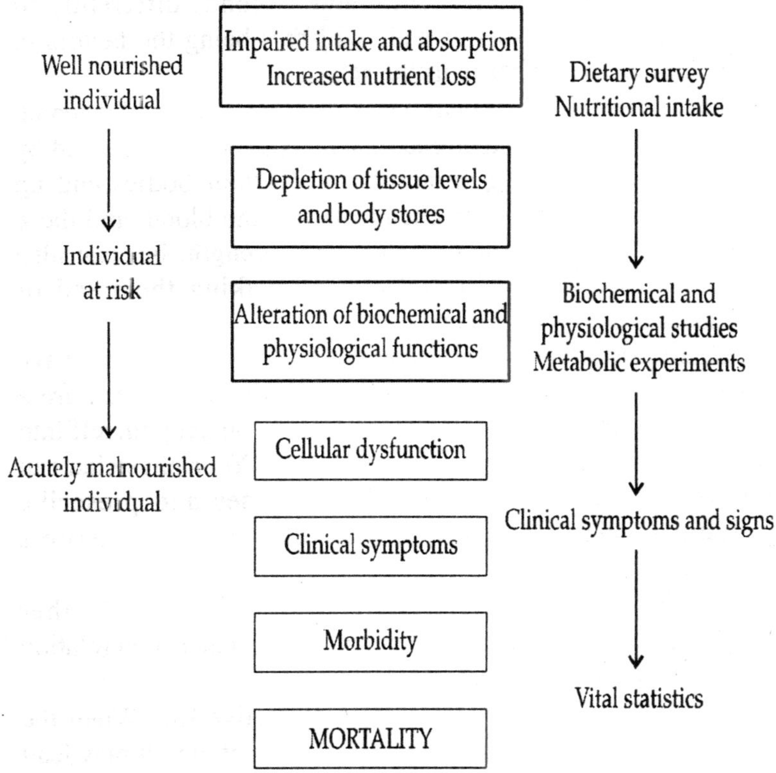

- Medication
- Consulting health care team
- Positive approach

Balanced diet: The diet which contains different types of food in such quantities and proportions that the needs for all the nutrients are adequately met.

To meet an individual's balanced diet, it is important to understand the concept of various foods that make diet plan or a balanced meal so that each component is rightly distributed and understood. The "Five Food Group System" helps in defining balanced diet components. The distribution is as follows:

Food Groups	*Main Nutrients*
1. Cereals—(staple diet) Rice, Wheat, Ragi, Bajra, Maize, Jowar, Riceflakes	Energy (Carbohydrate) Protein, B-complex vitamins, Iron, Fiber
2. Pulses and Legumes (veg. protein) All dals, Soyabean, Rajmah, Cowpea, Peas, Beans	Energy (Carbohydrate) Protein, B-complex vitamins, Iron, Calcium, Fiber
3. Milk and Milk products, (Animal protein) Milk, Curds, Paneer	Protein, Fat, Calcium, Vitamin B2,
Meat (animal protein) Chicken, Fish, Egg, Mutton	Protein, Fat, Calcium, Vitamin B2,
4. Fruits and Vegetables (dietary fiber)	Energy (Carbohydrate)
Fruits: Mango, Guava, Papaya, Orange, Melon	Vitamin C, Fiber
Veg (Green Leafy)—Spinach, Methi, Bathua	Vitam B Complex, Calcium, Iron, Fiber
Veg (Others)—Brinjal, Capsicum, Cauliflower	
5. Fats and Sugars (calories/energy)	
Fats: Oils, Butter, Ghee	Fat, Energy (calories)
Sugars : Sugar, Jaggary, Honey	Energy (Carbohydrate)

Importance of food group system

1. **Tool for nutritional assessment and screening**—A brief diet history system can disclose inadequacies of nutrient from any of the 5 groups. This information can be the first clue for the possibility of the subject may be at the risk of developing nutritional deficiency.
2. **Tool for nutritional counseling**—The dietary history based on 5 food group system allows a health team to counsel a patient about nutrition i.e. a diet plan.
3. **Explaining therapeutic diets to a patient**—Therapeutic (*Treatment and care to combat disease*) diets are scientifically based on nutrient composition and food groups which can be used in menu planning.

Generally, nutrients are divided into two classes: macronutrients and micronutrients.

Macro (major) nutrients are required daily in large quantities. They include proteins, fats, carbohydrates and water.

Micro (minor) nutrients are required daily in small quantities. They include vitamins and trace minerals that enable the body to use macronutrients.

Nutritional components of food.

Macronutrients—carbohydrates, proteins, fats, water.

Micro nutritients—vitamins and minerals

The nutritional requirements of all individuals vary from one another depending upon age, gender, physical activity, physiological stress or condition (e.g. pregnancy or lactation). For meeting the requirements the ICMR (Indian Council of Medical Research) has given.

Recommended Dietary Allowance (RDA)

- Average daily nutrient intake level that meets the needs of nearly all (97-98%) healthy people in a particular life stage and gender group.
- RDA are given for different groups: adults, infants, children, pregnant and lactating women.
- Takes into account individual variation in nutrient needs and availability for nutrients which may vary from diet to diet.

Meal Planning: Meal planning is planning what you are going to serve for a certain amount of time, could be a week, could be a day, and could be a month. It involves organizing the ingredients and recipes.

Principles of Meal Planning

- Meeting nutritional requirements—already discussed.
- Fulfill family needs—ensure that diet does not vary according to each member in family, rather it meets every ones needs when put together. For e.g. it is not advisable to plan 5 different kinds of meals for 5 members in breakfast or any meal, its importance to understand the distribution of macro and micro nutrients and then plan in common.
- Save time and energy—meals planned should not be time consuming.

- Economics—meal planning also involves meeting the financial condition of the individual or family. For e.g. if protein intake is not sufficient and the person can make changes in diet, it is not advisable to add supplements replacing diet and adding extra cost burden.
- Provide maximum nutrients.
- Likes and dislikes (veg./non-veg.)—it is very important to meet the likes and dislikes of the person. For e.g. Roti and dal cannot be prescribed to a person who is living in south India for all the meals.
- Variety—ensure that all nutrients are a part of diet plan, therefore adding variety, colour, flavour and most important there is no monotony in the plan.
- Satiety—it means distributing the meals in such a way that the person should not feel starved or dissatisfied with the portion size after the meal, i.e. meal should give a feeling of fullness but not over loading.

Macro Nutrients

Carbohydrates, proteins, and fats supply 90 per cent of the dry weight of the diet and 100 per cent of its energy. As sources of energy, carbohydrates, proteins, and fats are interchangeable in proportion to their energy content. The energy content is 4 calories in a gram of carbohydrate or protein and 9 calories in a gram of fat. However, these nutrients differ in how quickly they supply energy; carbohydrates are the quickest, and fats are the slowest.

Carbohydrates, proteins, and fats are digested in the intestine, where they are broken down into their basic units: carbohydrates into sugars, proteins into amino acids, and fats into fatty acids and glycerol. The body uses these basic units to build substances it needs for growth, maintenance, and activity (including other carbohydrates, proteins, and fats).

Carbohydrates: Energy producing compound that makes up about half of our food intake .1g CHO = 4 Kcal. These are a group of organic compounds, including sugars, starches and fiber.

Depending on the size of the molecule, carbohydrates may be **simple or complex.**

Simple carbohydrates are various forms of sugar. Because they are small molecules; they can be broken down by the body quickly and are the quickest source of energy.

Monosaccharide ("mono" = one + "saccharide" = sugar) is the simplest form of carbohydrate. Glucose, Fructose and Galactose are monosaccharides.

➢ **Glucose** is the chief end product of digestion of disaccharides and polysaccharides.
- It is found in sweet fruits such as grapes, berries and oranges and in some vegetables such as sweet corns and carrots.
- It is the form of carbohydrates circulating in the blood and it is utilized by the cell for energy.

➢ **Fructose** is also known as fruit sugar.
- It is found in honey, ripe fruits and some vegetables.

➢ **Galactose** is produced by the hydrolysis of lactose.

Food sources of simple carbohydrates include sugar, honey, refined flour, fruit juices, soft drink, cakes, cookies, chapatti, idli, noodles, plain rice etc.

Disaccharide ("di" = two + "saccharide" = sugar): made up of 2 single sugar units linked together

SUCROSE = GLUCOSE + FRUCTOSE
(Table Sugar) found in cane, beet root
LACTOSE = GLUCOSE + GALACTOSE
(Milk sugar)
MALTOSE = GLUCOSE + GLUCOSE
(present in beer and malted breakfast cereals)

Complex carbohydrates are composed of long strings of simple carbohydrates. Because complex carbohydrates are larger molecules than simple carbohydrates, they are slower sources of energy.

➢ Polysaccharide (more than one sugar): they don't taste sweet
- Starch—it is the storage form of carbohydrates in plants.
- Glycogen—it is the storage form of carbohydrates in humans and animals.
- Fiber—it is the indigestible form of carbohydrate, provide structure to plant.

- Dextrin—it is the breakdown product of long chains of starch during digestion.

Complex carbohydrates occur in wheat products (such as breads and pastas), other grains (such as rye and corn), beans, and root vegetables (such as potatoes).

The body stores very small amounts of excess energy as carbohydrates. The liver stores some as glycogen, a complex carbohydrate that the body can easily and rapidly convert to energy. Muscles also store glycogen, which they use during periods of intense exercise. The amount of carbohydrates stored as glycogen provides almost a day's worth of calories.

Functions of carbohydrates

- Main source of energy
- Excess of calories consumed in the form of carbohydrates are stored as fat in the adipose tissue
- Protein Sparing Effect
- Dietary fiber help relieve constipation
- Increases satiety (feeling of fullness)
- Delays glucose absorption
- Reduces serum cholesterol

Most authorities recommend that about 50 to 55 per cent of the total daily calories should consist of carbohydrates.

Fiber

Include all parts of plant food that body can't digest or absorb. Also known as roughage or bulk.

Dietary fiber can be classified in 2 forms:

1. Soluble fiber
2. Insoluble fiber

Soluble Fiber	*Insoluble Fiber*
It is the edible portion of plant foods, resistant to digestion and absorption in small intestine. While passing through large intestine (colon) partial or total fermentation occurs due to the action of colonic bacterial It dissolves in water to form a gel like substance.	It is made up of the structural material of the cell wall of plant foods It does not dissolve rather soaks up adding bulk to the stool, soften the stool and increases the transit time through the intestinal tract.
It lowers total and LDL (bad) cholesterol, reducing risk of heart disease. Regulates blood sugar levels in people with diabetes.	It promotes regular bowel movement and prevents constipation. Removes toxic waste material from the intestines faster. Gives satiety (a feeling of fullness), therefore, helps in weight loss.
Found in pulp of fruits, legumes, oats and greens.	Found in skin of various fruits, green vegetables, wheat bran.

Diabetes and Gastroparesis

- Gastroparesis, also called delayed gastric emptying, is a disorder in which the stomach takes too long to empty its contents.
- It often occurs in people with type 1 diabetes or type 2 diabetes.
- Gastroparesis happens when nerves to the stomach are damaged or stop working. The vagus nerve controls the movement of food through the digestive tract. If the vagus nerve is damaged, the muscles of the stomach and intestines do not work normally, and the movement of food is slowed or stopped.
- Diabetes can damage the vagus nerve if blood glucose levels remains high over a long period of time. High blood glucose causes chamical changes in nerves and damages the blood vessels that carry oxygen and nutrients of the nerves.

Signs and Symptoms of Gastroparesis in Diabetes

- Heartburn
- Nausea
- Vomiting of undigested food
- An early feeling of fullness when eating
- Weight loss
- Abdominal bloating
- Erratic blood glucose levels
- Lack of appetite

These symptoms may be mild or severe, varying from person to person.

Points to remember for dietary advise for Gastroparesis

√ Eat smaller, more frequent meal.
√ Low insoluble fiber foods.
√ Low fat diet.
√ Eat and drink all foods and beverages while sitting.
√ Solid foods are often better tolerated earlier in the day with a switch to semi solid or liquid meals later in the day.

Glycemic Index

➢ Glycemic Index is the ability of carbohydrates to raise the blood glucose.

➢ It is a quanlitative assessment of foods based blood glucose level after a meal.

➢ Per cent of the response to an equivalent CHO portion of a reference food.

➢ Reference food is white bread with GI set at 100.

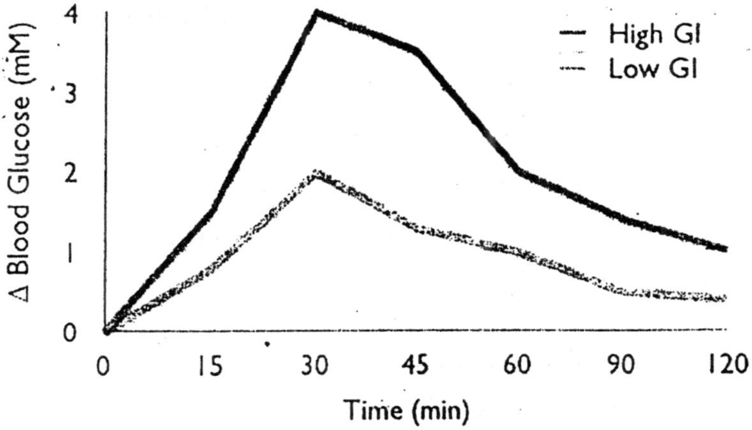

Effect On Blood Glucose From A High Vs Low Glycemic Index Carbohydrate

Factors affecting Glycemic Index

- **Size:** Grains that are in their original form like whole wheat and barley have a lower GI than other forms of these substances such as refined flours
- **Processing:** Pounding, mixing, grinding = Processing = decrease in particle size
  For e.g. Whole wheat—broken wheat (dalia)—semolina (suji)—refined wheat flour (maida)
- **Fiber content:** Fiber slows down the emptying of bowels, fiber will have a lower index.

Glycemic Load

- Glycemic load of a particular food is the product of the glycemic index of the food and the amount of carbohydrate in a serving
- By summing the glycemic load contributed by individual foods, the overall glycemic load of a meal or the whole diet can be calculated

How Glycemic Load is Calculated

The formula for calculating glycemic load is simple. Multiply the GI value of a food by the amount of carbohydrate per serving and divide the result by 100.

An apple has a GI value of 40

1. A serving (medium size apple) contains 15 grams of carbohydrate, (GI = 40)
   The glycemic load of an apple is: (40 × 15) = 600 divided by 100 = 600/100 = 6

Mixed fruit jam has a GI value of 51

2. Its p of jam (GI = 51) : (51 × 5 g jam)/100 = 2.5

GI and GL for Common Foods

Food	*GI*	*Serving Size*	*Net Carbs*	*GL*
Bean sprouts	25	1 cup	4	1
Grapefruit	25	½ large	11	3
Pizza	30	2 slices (med)	42	13
Low fat yogurt	33	1 cup	47	16
Apples	38	1 medium	16	6
Spaghetti	42	1 cup	38	16
Carrots	47	1 large	5	2
Oranges	48	1 medium	12	6
Banana	52	1 large	27	14
Potato chips	54	4 oz	55	30
Snickers Bar	55	1 bar	64	35
Brown rice	55	1 cup	42	23
Honey	55	1 tbsp	17	9
Oatmeal	58	1 cup	21	12
Ice cream	61	1 cup	16	10
Macaroni and cheese	64	1 serving	47	30
Raisins	64	1 small box	32	20
White rice	64	1 cup	52	33
Sugar (sucrose)	68	1 tbsp	12	8
White bread	100	1 slice	14	14
Watermelon	72	1 cup	11	8
Popcorn	72	2 cups	10	7
Baked potato	85	1 medium	33	28
Glucose	100	(50 g)	50	50

GI's of 55 or below are considered low, and 70 or above are considered high
GL's of 10 or below are considered low, and 20 or above are considered high.

Points to remember

- √ Eat at regular times
- √ Choose a variety of foods from all food groups
- √ Limit simple sugars
- √ Include food sources from complex carbohydrates in every main meal
- √ It is not only the quality (GI) but also the quantity (GL) of carbohydrates that is important in the meal plan.

Proteins: The word "protein" is derived from the Greek word "proteios", which means primary or holding first place. The way name suggest this group of components are the most important cell constituent. Protein is present in all cells of the body. It is present in variable level in different tissues of the body like muscles contain about 20 per cent where as in blood plasma it is 7 per cent.

Functions of Dietary Protein

1. Proteins are necessary structural integrity of cells and growth of the body.
2. They are required for the formation of enzymes, digestive juices, haemoglobin and hormones.
3. Required for the protection of the body against infection.
4. Proteins help in the transport of oxygen and nutrients.
5. Protein is required for tissue repair.
6. They are needed for the production of milk proteins during lactation.
7. To replace the daily loss of body proteins.

Proteins are also a source of energy (not desirable if protein is utilized for energy source then it will not be able to provide protection against infections and growth and repair which may lead to increased susceptibility to infections). Each gram of protein provides 4 kcal.

Therefore, when carbohydrates constitute to about 50 per cent of the dietary intake it is referred to as Protein Sparing action where in proteins are not utilized for giving energy to various cells of body. And protein can fulfill its functions.

Therefore, it is essential to have a balanced diet with all nutrients in required amounts, as per the individual.

Each protein in the body is tailored for a specific need, proteins are not interchangeable. Body cannot directly use proteins found in food. Dietary protein is broken down into its constituent amino acids, which the body then uses to build the different specific proteins it needs. It is the amino acids rather than protein that are the essential nutrients.

Amino Acids are the chemical units or "building blocks" of the body that make up proteins. There are 22 amino acids found in plant and animal proteins.

Essential Amino Acids: (9)

These can not be synthesized in the body, hence have to be obtained from the food.

Histidine, Isileucine, Leucine, Lysine, Methionine, Phenylalanine, Threonine, Tryptophan, Valine.

Non-Essential Amino Acid : (11)

These can be synthesized in the body, hence need not be obtained from the diet.

Alanine, Arginine, Aspartic Acid, Cystine, Glutamine, Glycine, Ornithine, Proline, Serine, Taurine, Tyrosine

Types of Protein

Dietary protein can be classfied in 2 forms:

1. Complete or Class 1 protein
2. Incomplete or Class 2 protein

Complete/Class 1 Protein	*Incomplete/Class 2 Protein*
√ Provide all EAA in adequate amounts and proportions needed by the body for growth and tissue maintenance	√ These are deficient in one or more EAA
√ Totally used by body and very little waste is left	√ Not completely used by the body and produce more waste products
√ Animal protein	√ Plant protein
√ Fish, chicken, eggs, meat and dairy products	√ Legumes, pulses, cereals, soybeans and nuts

➢ ***Nitrogen Balance:*** The difference between the dietary intake of nitrogen (mainly protein) and its excretion (as urea and other waste products)

Nitrogen Balance = N (intake) – N (excretion)

Healthy adults excrete the same amount as is ingested, and so are in Nitrogen equilibrium.

Positive Nitrogen Balance is a condition where the intake of protein increases its excretion or output.

Intake > Excretion

For e.g.: Pregnancy, lactation, growth, adequate protein intake

Negative Nitrogen Balance is a condition where the intake of protein is less than its excretion or output.

Excretion > Intake

For e.g. Malnourishment, burns, fever, injury, post-surgery, starvation, Inadequate protein intake

Protein quality : The most important function of dietary protein is to maintain body tissue and promote growth. Proteins differ in their capacity to maintain body tissue and promote growth. It depends upon the protein "quality".

Protein quality depends upon:

1. Whether or not the dietary protein supplies all 9 essential amino acids.
2. The ratio or the proportion of amino acids in the dietary proteins as compared to that needed in the body.

3. Digestibility: A measure of the amount of amino acids absorbed from a given dietary protein.

Improving protein quality **:** In general, **plant proteins are of lower quality** than animal proteins, and plants also provide **less protein per gram of food.**

Deficiency of an amino acid in one food item can be compensated for by combining it with another food item which has it in adequate amounts. This is known as **Mutual Supplementation.**

Complementary proteins provide all essential amino acids in quantities needed to support health.

Limiting amino acid: The amino acid that is found in shortest supply relative to the amount needed for the protein synthesis by the body. The most common limiting amino acids are:

Lysine → Grains

Methionine → Beans and Legumes

1. **Cereal Protein + Pulse Protein**
   Example: Idli or Dosa with Sambhar, Dhokla
   A combination of cereal and pulse in the ratio of 5 : 1 has been found to be given an optimum combination.
2. **Plant Protein + Animal Protein**
   Example: Dahi vada, Rice kheer, Curd rice

Points to remember**:** In general, proteins of uncooked vegetable foods (esp. pulses) are less digestible than those of animal foods.

Some pulses used in food contain chemical constituents having toxic properties.

TRYPSIN inhibitors proteins that inhibit the activity of TRYPSIN in the gut and interfere with the digestibility of dietary proteins and reduce their utilization. These are destroyed on cooking.

Soybean has a powerful trypsin inhibitor which is destroyed by dry roasting for 15-20 minutes. Therefore, cooking and heat treatment improves the digestibility of protein in several foods.

Protein deficiency: Lack of dietary protein may lead to following conditions:

- Stunted growth in children
- Muscle wasting
- Increased susceptibility to infection.
- Poor wound healing
- Anemia
- Edema

***RDA of Protein*:** Average daily protein requirement of an Indian adult is **1g/kg present body weight/day**

FATS—Fats are organic compounds that are made up of carbon, hydrogen, and oxygen; they are the most concentrated source of energy in foods. Fats belong to a group of substances called lipids. Fats come in liquid or solid form. All fats are combinations of saturated and unsaturated fatty acids. Fat provides 9 calories per gram, more than twice the number provided by carbohydrates or protein.

Functions of Fats: The functions of fats are as follows:

- Fat is the concentrated source of energy. 1g fat = 9 Kcal
- It is stored in the fat cells within the adipose (fat) tissue. Body fat provides the most important reservoir of stored energy as adipose tissue. Even in a person who is not overweight, body fat still makes up about 10 per cent of their body weight. From a survival standpoint, this is absolutely critical, since in periods of low food availability or during a famine situation, a person must live off his/her stored body fat or perish.
- Fat is a fairly poor conductor of heat, body fat in the subcutaneous tissues (under the skin) acts as insulation, and tends to prevent loss of body heat.
- Fat, in the form of structural body fat, provides important protection for the vital internal organs.
- These protective deposits are the last to be drawn on for energy supplies when energy in the diet is inadequate.
- It helps in transportation and use of fat soluble vitamins A, D, E, and K. Without fat in the diet, those vitamins would not be able to function. This would result in severe

problems with eyesight, skin, nail formation, blood clotting, kidney function, bone growth and repair, reproductive functions, and cellular energy.

Classification of Fats: Fats can be classified on the basis of their visibility and chemical structure.

Visibility	*Visible fats*	*Invisible fats*
Chemical Structure	Saturated fats Medium chain triglycerides	Unsaturated fats (a) Monounsaturated fats (b) Polyunsaturated fats

Classification of Fats depending on visibility

Visible fats	*Invisible fats*
They are visible to the naked eye. It	They are not visible to the naked eye but
includes all the fats and oils that are used for cooking.	add to the calories in the food. All foods contain invisible fats in varying amounts.
For e.g.: Butter, ghee, oils, vanaspati or dalda, processed cheese.	For e.g.: Cereals, pulses, dairy products, nuts, oilseeds, eggs, meats.

Classification of fats depending on chemical structure

1a. Saturated Fats—They are solid/semi-solid at room temperature, with the exception of certain oils. They are usually from animal sources.
e.g.: Ghee, butter, red meat, cheese, whole milk and products, coconut oil, palm oil (plant source).
They increases LDL (bad) cholesterol and reduces HDL (good) cholesterol and increases plasma triglycerides (TG) levels as well.

b. Medium Chain Triglycerides—These are saturated fatty acids, but with a slight difference in their structure. MCTs are more readily hydrolyzed and absorbed than conventional food fat. They require less enzymes and bile acids for digestion than conventional food fat. These are of use in patients suffering from pancreatic and liver disorders.

e.g.: Coconut oil, palm oil, butter and commercial products.

3. **Unsaturated Fats**—These are liquid at room temperature. These are commonly found in vegetables, nuts, and seeds. They help lower blood cholesterol level but amount consumed needs to be checked.
   There are two types: Mono-Unsaturated Fatty Acids (MUFAs) and Polyunsaturated Fatty Acids (PUFAs)—(a) Omega 3 (b) Omega 6.

Mono-Unsaturated Fatty Acids—Monounsaturated oils are liquid at room temperature but start to solidify at refrigerator temperatures. They are less susceptible to oxidation. They have favourable effect on blood lipids when consumed in moderate amounts. Helps decrease the level of LDL (bad) cholesterol.

For e.g.: olive oil, groundnut oil, rice bran oil, sesame oil, red palm oil.

Polyunsaturated Fatty Acids—Polyunsaturated oils are liquid at room temperature and in refrigerator as well. They easily combine with oxygen in the air to become rancid.

It includes omega 6 (linoleic) and omega 3 (linolenic) fatty acids, also called as **essential fatty acids**—The body cannot synthesize the essential fatty acids. They must be consumed in the diet.

Sources of Omega 6 fatty acids are corn oil, safflower oil, sesame oil (til), sunflower oil, soybean oil and cottonseed oil.

Sources of Omega 3 fatty acids are fish, fish oils, walnuts, flaxseeds, green leafy vegetables, soybean and rajma.

Studies have shown that *"Omega-3s" from fish are highly polyunsaturated fatty acids that lower triglycerides, reduce abnormal heart rhythms, reduce blood pressure by small but significant amounts, and improve blood clotting regulation.*

- ➢ Omega-3 fatty acids may be particularly beneficial for overweight people with hypertension who are on weight loss diets. Dr. Trevor Mori and colleagues at the University of Western Australia recently showed that people on a weight loss diet that included fat-rich fish daily had improved glucose and insulin metabolism.

➢ Japanese, who also consume large amounts of fish, have much lower rates of heart disease and diabetes than Americans.

The recommended ratio of omega 6 : omega 3 in diet is 4 : 1. Therefore, the oils that meet this recommendation are the preferred ones in the diet.

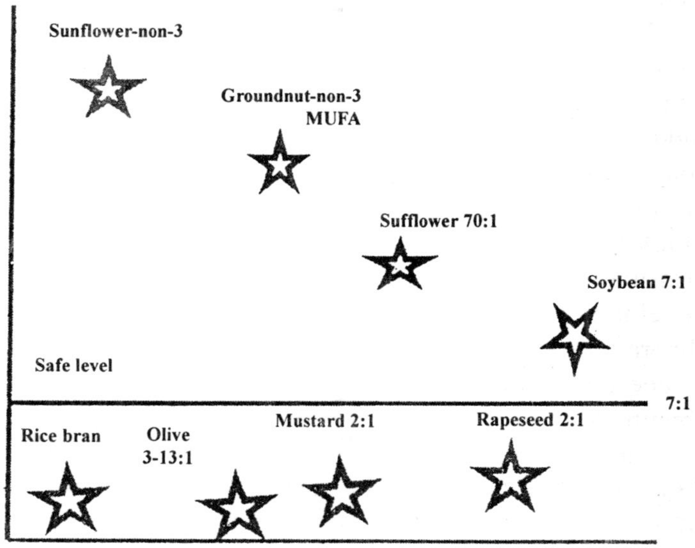

Recommended Ratio of n-6 to n-3 in diet is 4 : 1

Blood cholesterol: Cholesterol is a fat like substance in the blood. It is made in liver and we also get cholesterol from certain foods in our diet. Too much cholesterol can build up in arteries over a long period of time. Hypercholesterolemia is the term used for high levels of blood cholesterol. It can cause heart attacks and stroke.

There are 2 sources of cholesterol in our body.

1. **ENDOGENOUS cholesterol** is what our body makes (75%).
2. **EXOGENOUS cholesterol** is that which comes from diet (25%)

e.g. meat, poultry, fish egg yolk, butter, cheese and full cream milk and its products.

Note: Cholesterol is present only in animal foods

Lipoproteins are tiny spherical particles which circulate in the blood. They contain cholesterol, fat, and protein in varying amounts depending on where they are produced in the body and on the jobs they are directed to perform.

Abnormalities of the amounts or kinds of lipoproteins in blood can cause increased risk of atherosclerosis in the coronary arteries (leading to heart attack, angina or coronary pain, or sudden death) and atherosclerosis in many other arteries in the body. **Atherosclerosis is sometimes referred to as hardening or narrowing of the arteries, cholesterol deposition, or arterial blockage.** Other risk factors such as smoking, high blood pressure, diabetes, and sedentary lifestyle also contribute to the development of atherosclerosis. The risk from lipoprotein abnormalities can be especially severe, if a very high elevation of one type of lipoprotein is present, or if several lipoprotein abnormalities are found together in one person.

The total cholesterol level measures blood cholesterol in all lipoproteins combined. More specific measurements are LDL and HDL cholesterol. Triglyceride and lipoprotein(a) tests are explained below.

Low Density Lipoproteins (LDL) perform the task of moving cholesterol from the liver to sites where it is used in other tissues. An increased level of total cholesterol in blood usually indicates high LDL cholesterol, since most of the total cholesterol is normally found in LDL. LDL is sometimes called the "bad" cholesterol, since some of the LDL particles enter the walls of arteries, where they form harmful cholesterol deposits. The higher the level of LDL cholesterol in blood, the more likely a person will develop coronary or other atherosclerotic disease.

High Density Lipoproteins (HDL) carry approximately one-fouth of the total amount of cholesterol in blood. Studies have shown that persons who have more of their blood cholesterol in HDL, as opposed to other lipoproteins, will have fewer heart attacks and coronary deaths. One of the functions of HDL is reverse cholesterol transport—that is, the transport of cholesterol from body tissues back to the liver. These facts suggest that the HDL cholesterol level can serve as a rough measure of the blood's ability to regulate (and reduce) the cholesterol content of body tissues. Cholesterol in HDL has been called the "good cholesterol".

Body fat is triglyceride. Certain lipoproteins (chylomicrons and very low density lipoproteins—VLDL) perform the job of transporting fat in the blood. The triglyceride in these lipoproteins comes from both body fat and dietary fat. Triglyceride is eventually broken down into fatty acids, which are the major fuel used by the body to produce movement and heat and to energize other chemical processes. High levels of triglyceride-rich lipoproteins are generally associated with increased coronary risk.

Trans Fatty Acids : Trans fatty acids are the fats produced by heating liquid vegetable oil in the presence of hydrogen. The process is known as hydrogenation. They are used in commercial baked goods and for cooking in most restaurants and fast-food chains. They raise LDL and lower HDL. The sources of trans fats in the diet are bread, biscuits, pastries, puffs, vanaspati, margarine, commercially fried foods like french fries.

Dietary Approaches for Dealing with Increased Cholesterol

The Step I and Step II diets were created by the National Heart, Lung, and Blood Association's National Cholesterol Education Programme (NCEP). The American Heart Association endorsed them. Both diets were designed to reduce risk of cardiovascular disease by reducing high blood cholesterol levels.

Recommendation	*Step 1 diet*	*Step 2 diet*
Total fat	< 30% total calories	< 30% total calories
Saturated fat	< 10% total calories	< 7% total calories
MUFA	10-15% total calories	10-15% total calories
PUFA	< 10% total calories	< 10% total calories
Cholesterol	< 300 mg/day	< 200 mg/day

For people at high risk or who have known cardiovascular disease, AHA has adopted the Therapeutic Lifestyle Changes (TLC) diet. This is the "next generation" of the Step II diet recommended in May 2001. That's when the NCEP released new guidelines for cholesterol management.

Nutrient—Recommended Intake as Per cent of Total Calories:

- **Total Fat**—25–35%
- **Saturated Fat**—Less than 7%
- **Polyunsaturated Fat**—Up to 10%
- **Monounsaturated Fat**—Up to 20%
- **Carbohydrate**—50-60% of total calories
- **Protein**—Approximately 15%
- **Cholesterol**—Less than 200 mg per day
- **Total Calories**—Balance energy intake and expenditure to maintain desirable body weight and prevent weight gain.

  Reference: © 2008 American Heart Association.

Role of fat in the diet

1. **SOURCE OF ENERGY:** Fat is the most concentrated source of energy in the diet. **1g of Fat = 9 kcal**
2. **SATIETY VALUE:** Fat tends to leave the stomach relatively slowly. It is released from the stomach 3.5 hrs after a meal depending on the size and composition of the meal. This prolonged stay in the stomach helps to delay the onset of hugner and so contributes to a feeling of satiety after a meal.
3. **PALATABILITY:** The presence of fat in food or its addition to food is responsible for much of the texture and flavour of food.

Recommendations by ADA

Recommendations	*For Diabetes Patients*
Total cholesterol	<160 mg/dl
LDL cholesterol	<70 mg/dl
HDL cholesterol Men	>40 mg/dl
Women	>50 mg/dl
Triglycerides	<150 mg/dl

MICRONUTRIENTS

Definition of Micronutrient:

A substance, such as a vitamin or mineral, that is essential in minute amounts for the proper growth and metabolism of a living organism.

Vitamins

Although vitamins are necessary to maintain good health, they are neither sources of energy, nor significant contributors to the substance of the body. They act principally as regulators of metabolic processes. In general, none of them can be formed in the body—except niacin and vitamins A, D, and K. For those who are in relatively good health, adequate levels of the essential vitamins can be obtained through well-balanced diets.

Definition of Vitamin

An organic compound, essential in very small amounts in supporting normal physiologic function that cannot generally be biosynthesized at rates equivalent to the needs of the body.

Types of Vitamins

Water-Soluble

- soluble in water
- not stored in appreciable amounts

- regular consumption necessary
- excreted in the urine
- toxicity rare
- Ex: B-complex vitamins and Vitamin C

Fat-Soluble

- soluble in fat
- absorbed and transported with dietary lipids
- significant amounts stored in the liver
- can result in toxicity
- Ex: Vitamin A, D, E, K

Water-Soluble Vitamins:

- B-Complex Vitamins: These include the following:

√ Thiamine (vitamin B1)
√ Riboflavin (vitamin B2)
√ Niacin
√ Pantothenic acid
√ Pyriodoxine (vitamin B6)
√ Biotin
√ Folic acid
√ Vitamin B12

All B-complex vitamins play an important part of key reactions of the metabolic processes in the body. They help in the conversion of food (CHO proteins, fats) to energy; hence thier requirements are energy-related.

Below is a table enlisting the food sources of important vitamins along with the causes of losses of these vitamins from the food.

Vitamin	*Major Food Sources*	*Causes of Losses*
Thiamine (B1)	Yeast, liver, cereal grains, nuts	Milling, refining, heat, excessie washing, baking, vigorous boiling, dehydration, overcooking, use of cooking soda
Riboflavin (B2)	Meat and dairy products, eggs, green leafy vegetables, soyabean	Use of baking soda, sun drying, cooking/boiling in excess water, milling of rice and wheat
Niacin	Meat, peanuts, dairy products, eggs, fish, whole grains, legumes	Grain processing
Pyridoxine (B6)	Whole grain foods (esp wheat), meats, veg, nuts	
Folic acid	Green leavy veg, organ meats, oranges (Bio-availability is 25-50%)	Easily oxidised during storage, cooking, processing at high temperatures.
Vitamin B12	Seafood, meat and meat products, fish, eggs. Strict vegetarians more prone to deficiency	Pasteurization and evaporation of milk

Vitamin C

Vitamin C (ascorbic acid) is a water-soluble vitamin important in the synthesis of collagen (necessary for wound healing) and in the maintenance of healthy gums and teeth. It is abundant in most fresh fruit and vegetables.

Some important functions of vitamin C are:

- **Antioxidant:** Exposure to drugs, environmental pollutants and stress results in the formation of oxidative agents in the body (oxidative stress). Vitamin C converts these oxidizing agents to harmless substances that can be excreted. It can combine with and scavenge all these free radicals and thus protect the body from damage. Free radicals are highly reactive chemicals that attack molecules by capturing electrons and thus modifying chemical structures.
- **Absorption of Iron and Calcium:** Vitamin C helps keep iron and calcium in soluble forms thus enhancing their

absorption. Hence, a source of vitamin C should always accompany an iron or calcium rich dish.

***Sources*:** Include citrus fruits like amla, orange, guava; green leafy vegetables (drumstick leaves, spinach); tomatoes, capsicum; sprouted pulses. Animal foods **DO NOT** contain vit C. Raw fresh foods are better sources of vit C than cooked foods.

Vitamin C is easily destroyed by oxidation, light, alkali and heat. Some of the common causes of losses of vitamin C are:

- Removal of skin/peel of fruits/vegetables will cause vit C to leach into the water used for cooking.
- Cutting food into small pieces and then cooking, increases losses due to increased surface area exposed to water and heat. Hence, cook whole.
- Use of copper cooking vessels destroys the vitamin.
- Use of large amount of water.
- Use of cooking soda.

Vitamin A:

It exists in 2 forms; Retinol form is present in animal foods and beta carotene is present in plant foods. Beta-carotene is a pigment in vegetables that gives them their yellow, orange or red colour. Once consumed, it is slowly converted to vitamin A (retinol) in the body. Only 50 per cent is absorbed and out of the absorbed only 50 per cent is converted to retinol.

It is essential for sound skin, tooth and bone health and development; it is also important in immune system function and the prevention of night blindness. Like vitamin C, it also plays the role of an antioxidant.

Major food sources of retinol are liver, fish oils, eggs, ghee, butter, milk and that of beta carotene are dark green leafy vegs, yellow and orange fruits and vegetables like carrots, papaya, mango and egg yolk. In an Indian diet, beta carotene provides most of the vitamin A necessary in human nutrition.

Vitamin A is lost from the food by deep-fat frying, by the use of defatted/low fat milk, oxidation and exposure to light. Malabsorption of fats, cholesterol-lowering drugs, and high fiber intake affect vit A absorption in the body.

Vitamin D

It is also known as the "sunshine vitamin". It is synthesised in the body by exposure to sunlight.

Two forms of vitamin D are important for nutrition:

- **Vitamin D_2 (ergocalciferol):** This form is synthesized from plants and yeast precursors. It is also the form used in very high dose supplements.
- **Vitamin D_3 (cholecalciferol):** This form is the most active form of vitamin D. It is formed in the skin when the skin is exposed to direct sunlight. The most common food source is fortified foods, mainly cereals and dairy products. Vitamin D_3 is also present in fish liver oils and fatty fish. Cholecalciferol serves as a precursor to the hormonal form 1,25-dihydroxyvitamin D3 (calcitriol).

Vitamin D is sotred mainly in the liver. Vitamin D_2 and D_3 are not active in the body. Both forms must be processed (metabolized) by the liver and kidneys into an active form called calcitriol. This active form promotes absorption of calcium and phosphorus from the intestine.

Functions:

1. Regulates the ***calcium and phosphorus*** levels in the blood by promoting their absorption from food in the intestines, and by promoting re-absorption of calcium in the kidneys.
2. It ***promotes bone formation*** and mineralization and is essential in the development of an intact and strong skeleton.

3. It ***inhibits parathyroid hormone*** secretion from the parathyroid gland.
4. Affects the ***immune system*** by promoting phagocytosis (The process by which a cell engulfs particles such as bacteria, other microorganisms, aged red blood cells, foreign matter, etc.), anti-tumor activity, and immunomodulatory functions.

Sources: Endogenous production is the most important source. Vitamin D occurs naturally in animal foods. The richest source is fish liver oils like cod liver oil and small amounts are present in fatty fish, butter, cream, egg yolk and liver.

Deficiency: In vitamin D deficiency, calcium and phosphate levels in the blood decrease because vitamin D is necessary for absorption of these minerals. Because not enough calcium and phosphate are available to maintain healthy bones, vitamin D deficiency may result in a bone disorder called rickets in children or ostemalacia and osteoporosis in adults. Vitamin D deficiency makes osteoporosis worse. To try to increase the low calcium level in blood caused by vitamin D deficiency, the body may produce more parathyroid hormone. However, as the parathyroid hormone level becomes high (a condition called hyperparathyroidism), the hormone draws calcium out of bone to increase the calcium level in blood. Thus, the bones are weakened.

The most common cause is inadequate exposure to sunlight. Thus, vitamin D deficiency occurs mainly among people who do not spend much time outdoors.

Vitamin D and Diabetes

Study 1: Vitamin D deficiency Predisposes Individuals to Type 1 and 2 diabetes.

Vitamin D deficiency predisposes individuals to type 1 and type 2 diabetes, and receptors for its activated form—1α, 25-dihydroxyvitamin D3—have been identified in both beta cells and immune cells. Vitamin D deficiency has been shown to impair insulin synthesis and secretion in humans and in animal models of diabetes, suggesting a role in the development to type 2 diabetes.

Study 2: Vitamin D and Calcium Intake in Relation to Type 2 Diabetes in Women

Vitamin D deficiency is associated with insulin resistance and impaired pancreatic beta cell function has been proved in some studies.

Vitamin E

Vitamin E (tocopherol) is an antioxidant: It protects cells against damage by free radicals and also prevents oxidation of LDL cholesterol thus playing a role in prevention of CVD.

Its utilisation depends upon presence of dietary fat and it is lost by deep fat frying.

A very low fat diet lacks vitamin E because vegetable oils are the main source of this vitamin. Other sources of this vitamin are nuts, wheat germ, green leafy vegetables, eggs, liver and muscle meats. Disorders that impair fat absorption can also reduce the absorption of vitamin E and increase the risk of vitamin E deficiency.

Requirement of vitamin E increases as PUFA intake increases and since dietary fats contain vit E, dietary deficiency is unlikely.

Vitamin K

Vitamin K has two forms:

- **Phylloquinone:** This form occurs in plants and is consumed in the diet. It is absorbed better when it is consumed with fat.
- **Menaquinone:** This form is produced by bacteria in the intestine, but only small amounts of it can be

absorbed. In some countries, this form is used for supplementation.

Vitamin K is necessary for the synthesis of the proteins that help control bleeding (clotting factors) and thus for the normal clotting of blood. It is also needed for healthy bones and other tissues.

Sources include green leafy vegetabels (content proprotional to chlorophyll content), soya oil, cottonseed oil and olive oil.

MINERALS

Sodium

Most of the body's sodium is located in the blood and in the fluid in the space surrounding the cells (ECF). Sodium is required by all cells in the body to maintain a normal fluid balance. Sodium plays a key role in normal nerve and muscle function. It is taken in through food and drink and lost primarily in sweat and urine. Healthy kidneys maintain a consistent level of sodium in the body by adjusting the amount excreted in the urine.

Some important functions are as follows:

1. Maintains water balance (major electrolyte in ECF)
2. Maintains BP
3. Transmission of nerve impulses and muscle contractions
4. Transport of sugar and amino acids (Na/K/Ca ATPase pump).

***Sources*:** Salt, bakery products, processed foods like cornflakes, pizzas, ajinomoto, cheese, salted butter, packet soups, pickles, papad, sauces and ketchups, namkeen like sev, chivda, wafers, chips, salted nuts, salted popcorn, fast foods, cooking soda, baking soda (1 tsp = 1000 mg sodium), dried sea food, some drugs like some antacids and laxatives.

- Table salt is 40 per cent sodium;
  1 tsp of table salt = 2,400 mg of sodium.
- ADA recommends sodium intake of less than 2400 mg/day (i.e. 1 tsp of salt/day)
- **Normal serum sodium = 135-145 meq/L**

Hyponatremia

In hyponatremia, the level of sodium in the blood is too low (<135 meq/l). Hyponatremia occurs when sodium has been overdiluted in the body. Sodium can be overdiluted when people drink enormous amounts of water and as a result the amount of fluid taken in exceeds the kidneys' capacity to eliminate the excess. Other reasons could be diarrhea, vomiting, burns, use of diuretics or extremely low intake.

Symptoms include loss of appetite, nausea, vomiting, headache, fatigue, irritability, lethargy, confusion, muscle twitching, seizures and coma.

Hypernatremia

In hypernatremia, the level of sodium in the blood is too high (>145 meq/l). The body contains too little water relative to the amount of sodium. The sodium level in the blood becomes abnormally high when water loss exceeds sodium loss, as occurs with dehydration. In most people, hypernatremia results from dehydration.

Hypernatremia occurs in people who drink too little water and in those who have diarrhea, vomiting, fever, excessive sweating (particularly during hot weather), or abnormal kidney function. Symptoms include dizziness due to hypotension, vomiting, diarrhea, edema.

Ways to Lower Sodium Intake:

1. Cook without added salt; use the prescribed amount of salt separately.

2. Add little or no salt at the table.
3. Read labels, looking for sodium content.
4. Choose fresh, frozen food items without added salts.
5. Select unsalted nuts.
6. Avoid salty snacks, like chips and namkeen.
7. Select unsalted soups or make them fresh at home.
8. Avoid junk foods, cooking soda, bakery products and processed foods.
9. Select fat-free or low-fat milk, low-sodium, low-fat cheeses, as well as low-fat curd.
10. Ask for your dish to be prepared without salt and/or ajinomoto when dining out.
11. Use spices and herbs to enhance the taste of your food; ex. Lime, tamarind, tomato, vinegar, ginger, garlic, mint.

Potassium

Most of the body's potassium is located inside the cells (ICF). Potassium is necessary for the normal functioning of cells, nerves, and muscles.

The level of potassium in the blood must be maintained within a narrow range. A potassium level that is too high or too low can have serious consequences, such as an abnormal heart rhythm or even cardiac arrest.

Kidney is the major excretory organ for potassium. Normal Serum potassium = 3.5 meg/l.

Some important functions are as follows:

1. Maintains water balance
2. Nerve impulse transmission and muscle contraction
3. Regulation of BP.
4. Required for normal growth and muscle building.

Sources are green leafy vegetables, fruits like sweet lime, chiku, watermelon, mango, cherries, litchis, peach, fruit juices and vegetable soups, coconut water, fresh or dry coconut, pulses and legumes, potato with skin, milk and milk products.

Hypokalemia

In hypokalemia, the level of potassium in the blood is too low (<3.5 meq/l). Excessive potassium loss usually results from vomiting, diarrhea and chronic laxative use. Very occasionally, excessive loss results from excessive sweating in conditions of extreme heat and humidity. Many foods contain potassium, so hypokalemia is rarely caused by too little intake in people who eat a balanced diet.

There are several reasons why potassium may be lost in the urine. By far the most common is the use of diuretics that cause the kidneys to excrete excess sodium, water, and potassium.

A mild decrease in the potassium level in the blood usually causes no symptoms. A more severe decrease can cause loss of appetite, mood changes, hypertension, loss of GI tone, elevated blood sugar, muscle weakness, twitches, and even paralysis. Abnormal heart rhythms may develop, especially in people with heart disease.

Hyperkalemia

In hyperkalemia, the level of potassium in the blood is too high. Hyperkalemia usually results when the kidneys do not excrete enough potassium. It can also result when a large amount of potassium is suddenly released from the cells. A sudden release of potassium from the cells can result from crush injuries (involving the destruction of large amounts of muscle tissue) and severe burns. The rapid movement of potassium from the cells into the bloodstream can overwhelm the kidneys and result in life-threatening hyperkalemia.

Other causes include GI bleed, severe infection, high intake of salt substitutes and use of potassium-sparing diuretics.

Symptoms include irregular heart beat (heart attack), nausea, slow/weak pulse.

Low potassium fruits include Guava, Apple, Pear, Papaya, Pineapple, Jamun, Orange, Banana (moderate)

Calcium

Most of the body's calcium is stored in the bones, but calcium is also found in cells (particularly muscle cells) and in the blood. Calcium is essential to muscle contraction and to the normal functioning of many enzymes. It is necessary for the formation of bone and teeth, for blood clotting, and for normal heart rhythm.

The body precisely controls the amount of calcium in the cells and the blood. Calcium content in the blood plasma is maintained within the narrow range of 9-11 mg/dl. Maintaining a normal level of calcium in the blood depends on consuming at least 1,000 to 1,500 milligrams of calcium a day and excreting excess calcium in urine. Calcium moves out of the bones into the bloodstream as needed to maintain a steady level of calcium in the blood. However, mobilizing too much calcium from the bones weakens them and can lead to osteoporosis.

Functions

1. Bone Formation: The important minerals within bone are calcium, phosphorus and magnesium.
2. Tooth Formation
3. Growth
4. Blood Clotting (Factor 4)
5. Regulates muscle contraction
6. Nerve impulse conduction
7. Co-factor necessary for many enzyme reactions:

a. Absorption of vitamin B12
b. In the action of fat digesting enzyme, pancreatic lipase.
c. In the **secretion of insulin from the pancreas**

Sources include dairy products (richest source), dark green leafy vegetables like colocassia (patra) leaves, cauliflower greens, amaranth (laal maath) leaves, cow pea (chawli) leaves, methi, lettuce, Ragi, legumes, almonds, black til, ravas, soybean and its products like tofu, soya milk.

Factors that enhance calcium absorption

1. Acid
2. Normal gastrointestinal motility
3. Phosphorus
4. Vitamin D
5. Need for calcium
6. Lactose
7. PTH

1. Acid

Calcium is more soluble and easily absorbed in acidic conditions.

2. GI motility

Normal motility of the GIT favours calcium absorption.

3. Phosphorus

An increase in the amount of phosphate in the diet results in a reduction in the amount of calcium excreted. There is an inverse relationship between the dietary phsphorus intake and urinary calcium.

4. Vitamin D

The presence of the active form of vitamin D can result in a 10-30 per cent increase in dietary calcium absorption.

Low vitamin D intakes or inadequate exposure to sunlight reduce calcium absorption, especially among the elderly.

5. Need for calcium

During pregnancy, lactation and adolescence when calcium needs are greatest absorption efficiency is as high as 50 per cent.

Also, when calcium intakes are low, the body adapts by absorbing a greater proportion of the dietary calcium available and excreting less.

6. Lactose

The lactose in breast milk improves calcium absorption in human infants.

Beyond infancy it is doubtful whether lactose improves the absorbability of calcium from dairy products.

7. Parathyroid Hormone (PTH)

PTH helps maintain normal serum calcium.

Low serum calcium stimulates the release of PTH, which in turn promotes increased intestinal absorption of calcium *via* activated vitamin D.

Factors that hinder calcium absorption

1. Inadequate vitamin D intake
2. Alkaline conditions
3. Impaired GI motility
4. Imbalance in calcium phosphorus ratio
5. Phytic and oxalic acid
6. Excessive use of laxatives
7. Steatorrhea.
8. High fiber intake
9. Lack of exercise
10. Ageing
11. Caffeine
12. Drugs
13. Excessive sodium intake
14. High intake of zinc, iron or magnesium.

15. Excessive intake of alcohol
16. Smoking
17. Stress
18. Fat malabsorption

5. Phytates and Oxalates

Phytic acid present in cereals prevents calcium absorption by forming an insoluble complex with calcium.

Foods rich in phytates include whole grain cereals like bajra, jowar, whole wheat flour, ragi, pulses and legumes.

Fermentation, as occurs during bread making, reduces phytic acid because of the phytase present in yeast.

Oxalic acid present in spinach forms an insoluble complex with calcium (calcium-oxalate) which cannot be absorbed. Only 5 per cent of the calcium in spinach is absorbed.

Other foods containing oxalates are chocolate, cocoa, tea, amaranth, beer, juices containing berries (rasberry/strawberry), dried figs, whole wheat bread, wheat germ, roasted peanuts, til seeds.

6. Excessive use of laxatives

Laxatives increase the rate of passage of food through the intestinal tract. This decreases calcium absorption by reducing the time available for the absorption to occur.

7. Steatorrhea

During steatorrhea (large foul smelling stools containing unabsorbed fat) calcium absorption is certainly reduced. This is because the malabsorbed fat forms insoluble soaps with calcium, preventing its absorption.

8. High fiber intake

Fiber reduces the absorption of calcium and other minerals by increasing the rate of passage of food through the intestinal tract.

This decreases calcium absorption by reducing the time available for the absorption to occur. It also binds minerals within the structure thus making them unavailable for absorption. (only if > 30 g/d).

9. Lack of exercise

People who do not engage in weight-bearing exercises, such as walking, and bed-ridden people who are essentially immobile, can lose as much as 0.5 per cent of bone in a month and have a reduced ability to replace it. This may an important cause of calcium loss and decreased bone strength and mass in old people.

10. Ageing

Calcium absorption is decreased during old age. This may be due to lack/inadequate amount of hydrocholoric acid in the stomach and/or inadequate exposure to sunlight, increasing the risk of fractures.

11. Excessive sodium intake

Sodium and calcium excretion are linked in the proximal tubule of the kidney. Excess sodium can increase calcium excretion. Each gram of sodium leads to the urinary excretion of about 15 mg of calcium when calcium intake is high or moderate.

12. Caffeine

High intakes of caffeine affect the bio-availability of calcium by increasing the loss of calcium in urine. Daily consumption of the amount of caffeine in 3.5 cups of coffee or 7 cups of tea, has been shown to almost double the risk of developing osteoporosis.

13. Drugs

Some medications like anticoagulants, cortisone and thyroxine reduce calcium absorption as a side effect.

14. Excess intake of Fe, zinc or mg

They share the same absorption pathway with calcium. Hence, excessive intakes of these minerals results in a competition between them for absorption.

15. Excessive alcohol intake

Drinking an average of 3 or more alcoholic drinks per day is clearly associated with an increased risk of osteoporosis. It has been well-established that even small doses of alcohol interfere with the absorption and use of both calcium and vitamin D.

16. Smoking

Greater incidence of osteoporosis was found among smokers than non-smokers.

17. Stress

Stress is also known to interfere with the body's ability to absorb minerals, including calcium.

18. Fat malabsorption

Calcium absorption is decreased because of the formation of calcium-fatty acid soaps.

RDA: 400 mg/d

IRON

There are two major pools of iron in the human body:

1. **Functional Iron:** Haemoglobin, myoglobin and enzymes.
2. **Storage Iron:** Ferritin, hemosiderin and transferrin.

Daily losses of iron are through GIT, skin, urine and menstrual losses.

Food contains two types of iron: heme iron (found in animal products) and non-heme iron (found in plant foods and in iron supplements). Non-heme iron accounts for more than 85 per cent of iron in the average diet. However, less than 20 per cent of non-heme iron that is consumed is absorbed into the body. Non-heme iron is absorbed better when it is consumed with animal protein and with vitamin C. Heme iron is absorbed much better than non-heme iron.

Functions:

1. Enables the transport of oxygen from lungs to the tissues.
2. Stores oxygen in muscle tissue.
3. Co-factor of many enzymes which carry out several vital functions in the body.
4. Essential for a healthy immune system and mental function.

Sources: Richest animal source is liver followed by oysters, seafoods, lean meat, poultry, egg yolk and fish. Plant sources include dark green leafy vegetables like amaranth, cauliflower greens, til seeds.

Iron Absorption from Indian Diets

- Adult men, children and adolescent boys—3 per cent
- Women, lactating women and adolescent girls—5 per cent
- Pregnant women—8 per cent

Factors increasing absorption are as follows:

1. Vitamin C
2. Acidic pH of the intestinal contents
3. Body need
4. Meat protein factor
5. Increased intestinal motility

1. *Vitamin C*

It is the most potent enhancer of iron absorption. It forms a chelate with iron that remains soluble at the alkaline pH of the lower small intestine. It enhances non-heme iron absorption especially well in women with low iron intakes.

2. *Acidic pH of the intestinal contents*

It keeps iron in the soluble form and improves bio-availability.

3. *Body's need*

During pregnancy and growth, which demand increased blood formation, there is increased iron absorption. In iron-deficiency anemia also, more iron is absorbed.

4. *Meat protein factor*

Animal proteins from pork, lamb, liver, fish and chicken enhance absorption. Substance responsible is known as the "Meat Protein Factor" (MPF). Mechanism unknown.

5. *Increased intestinal motility*

It decreases contact time. It rapidly removes the chyme from the area of highest intestinal acidity.

Factors that decrease absorption:

1. Phytates (*form insoluble complexes*)
2. Oxalates (*form insoluble complexes*)
3. Tannins
4. Dietary fiber (*increases transit time and acts as binder*)
5. Excess intake of zinc, manganese, calcium taken as supplements. (*absorption competition*)
6. Lack of stomach acid (*Makes non-hame iron insoluble*)
7. Antacids.

Iron Deficiency

Iron deficiency is the most common mineral deficiency in the world, causing anemia in men, women, and children.

In adults, iron deficiency is most commonly caused by loss of blood. In premenopausal women, monthly menstrual bleeding may cause the deficiency. Other causes are inadequate intake and malabsorption.

When iron reserves in the body are exhausted, anemia develops. Anemia causes paleness, weakness, irritability, drowsiness, and fatigue. Concentration and learning ability may be impaired. When severe, anemia may cause headache, ringing in the ears (tinnitus), spots before the eyes, digestive upset, shortness of breath, dizziness, and a rapid heart rate. Occasionally, severe anemia causes chest pain and heart failure. Menstrual periods may stop.

RDA: 30mg/d

Exchange List

Exchange	*Amount (g)*	*Calories (Kcal)*	*CHO (gms)*	*Protein (gms)*	*Fat (gms)*	*Fibre (mg)*
Cereal	30	100	21	2.5	0.5	0.6
Pulse	30	100	17	7	0.5	1.5
Cow's milk	100	70	4	3.2	4	—
Buffallo's milk	100	117	5	4.3	6.5	—
Mutton	50	100	—	8	7	—
Egg	1 no.	85	—	6.5	6.5	—
Fish or chicken	100	100	—	20.0	2.0	—
Vegetable A	100	25	6	1.0	—	1.2
Vegetable B	100	50	10	1.0	0.5	0.8
Vegetable C	100	100	24	1.0	—	0.7
Fruit	100	50	10	—	—	1.75
Soyabean	20	90	4	9	4	0.7
Sugar	5	20	5	—	—	—
Fat (1 tsp)	5	45	—	—	5	—
Coconut (dry)	15	100	2.5	1.02	10	0.9
Coconut (fresh)	25	100	3.0	1.12	10.4	0.9
Groundnut	15	100	8.0	3.79	6.0	0.5
Marie biscuit	4 no.	60				
Glucose biscuit	3 no.	110				

Edible Portions of Coconut

Coconut (Edible Portion)	*Fresh*	*Dry*
Small	175 g	—
Big	250 g	—
Standard	—	80 g.

Fuit Exchanges for Diabetic Patients

All fuits in the exchange list provide 10g CHO

Apple	1 small/½ medium
Guava	1 medium
Orange	1 medium
Papaya	1/3 medium or 3 slices = 12-14 pc "cube
Pineapple	2-3 slices
Pear	1 medium
Sweet lime	1 medium
Water melon	2-3 slices
Pomegranate	1/3rd medium
Coconut water	150 ml
Jamun	100 gm
High Calorie Fruits	
Banana	½ big
Mango	½ medium (75 g)
Chickoo	1 small
Sitaphal	(50g) ½ big size
Grapes	12-15 pieces

Thumb Rules for Making a Diet Plan

- **Time**
  Minimum 3 hrs gap between two major meals
- **Cereals**
  Rule:

  Reduction

  √ Total cereal exchanges no < 6/day

  √ Balance each meal

  √ Potato = cereal

- **PULSES**
  - √ 2.5 exchanges of pulses/day (ncluding soya)
  - √ Min of 1 exchange each in lunch and dinner
  - √ Max 1 exchange can be replaced 2-3 times/wk with:
  - √ Low fat paneer—1 med k *OR*
  - √ Egg whites—2 no. *OR*
  - √ Fish/Chicken-2 pieces.
- **FRUITS**
  - √ Permitted no. of fruit exchanges/day = 2
  - √ Food and fruit gap to be 2 hours.
- **FAT**
  - √ Visible fat allowance = 3-5 t/d (15-25 g/d)
- **SUGAR, JAGGERY AND HONEY**
  - √ Completely avoid.
- **MILK AND PRODUCTS**
  - √ Convert to low fat versions like toned/double toned/skimmed cow milk/skim milk.
  - √ Even paneer and curds to be made from the same low fat milk.
- **NON-VEG**
  - √ Egg whites, fish and chicken acceptable
  - √ Grilled, roasted, boiled, onion-tomato gravy-mode of cooking.
  - √ Red meat to be completely avoided
- **NUTS AND OILSEEDS**
  - √ Stop coconut (fresh, dry and milk), til and groundnut intake completely.
- **ALCOHOL**
  - √ Advice to stop
  - √ Reduce frequency and quantity by half
- **MISCELLANEOUS**
  - √ No bed-time snacks
  - √ Pre-exercise/walk: 1 cup milk/coffee, 1 excahnge fruit, 1 fistful kurmura-channa
  - √ Mid-meal snacks to be protein-rich
  - √ Salt allowance—1 leveled teaspoon/day.
  - √ Avoid/Replace junk food with healthier options

√ Follow Dr's advice regarding timing of medicine consumption.

Notes on Medical Nutrition Therapy for Diabetes

Diabetes mellitus is a chronic disease, without a cure, and medical emphasis must necessarily be on managing/avoiding possible short-term as well as long-term diabetes-related problems. There is an exceptionally important role for patient education, dietetic support, regular exercise, self glucose monitoring, with the goal of keeping both short-term blood glucose levels, and log-term levels as well, within acceptable bounds.

Management of diabetes involves 5 important pillars. These include:

1. **Medication**—It includes both oral medicines and insulin depending on the patient's stage of diabetes and doctor's prescription. It is extremely important to follow the doctor's advice for the same.
2. **Medical Nutrition Therapy**—Medical Nutrition Therapy (MNT) is a medically necessary and cost effective way of treating and controlling many diseases and medical conditions. It involves the assessment of nutritional status followed by therapy. It is integral to total diabetes care and management.
3. **Exercise**—Exercise can be defined as physical activity that is a planned, structured movement of the body designed to enhance physical fitness.
4. **Monitoring**—A way of testing how much glucose (sugar) is in the blood. It can be done at the lab and also at home using a device called glucometer. The process of monitoring blood sugars at home is known as Self Monitoring of Blood Glucose (SMBG).

SMBG can aid in diabetes control by:

- facilitating the development of an individualized blood glucose profile, which can then guide health care professionals in treatment planning for an individualized diabetic regimen;

- giving people with diabetes and their families the ability to make appropriate day-to-day treatment choices in diet and physical activity as well as in insulin or other agents;
- improving patients' recognition of hypoglycemia or severe hyperglycemia;
- enhancing patient education and patient empowerment regarding the effects of lifestyle and pharmaceutical intervention on glycemic control.

5. **Lifestyle**—It involves a person's pattern of living as expressed by their interests, motivations, activities, desired experiences, and beliefs. For e.g. intake of alcohol, smoking is one of the components of lifestyle and affects the blood sugars. Therefore, lifestyle management is also one of the important pillars for managing diabetes.

Role of MNT in diabetes: MNT like in any other condition performs the following role:

a. Encompasses clinical principles—it includes the clinical principles or guidelines that are to be followed. For e.g. 1 g protein/kg present wt.
b. Individual circumstances—it means that MNT takes into individual circumstances not by applying the same norms to everyone as each one of us is different.
c. Cultural and ethnic preferences—like-wise our circumstances, there is a variation in cultural and ethnic backgrounds. Therefore, MNT is flexible.
d. Maintains lifestyle changes—as discussed earlier lifestyle modification has an important role to play in DM management. Therefore it is an integral part of MNT.

Goals of MNT for Diabetes

- To attain and maintain optimal metabolic outcomes, including
  - — Blood glucose levels in the normal range.
  - — Lipid and lipoprotein profile that reduces the risk for vascular disease—levels of LDL, HDL, TG within the range.
  - — Blood pressure levels in the normal range or as close to normal as is safely possible.
- To prevent, or at least slow, the rate of development of chronic complications of diabetes—nutrient and lifestyle modification.
- To address individual nutritional needs, taking into consideration personal, cultural preferences and lifestyle.
- To maintain the pleasure of eating by only limiting food choices when indicated by scientific evidence.—entire diet of the patient should not be changed. The modifications made should hold a scientific basis. For e.g. a patient has T. Cholesterol—300 mg/dl and his consumption of SFAs is high. Therefore, his intake of SFAs needs to be restricted.

Insulin secretagogues are medicines that work by making the body produce more insulin from the pancreas. (Insulin in the hormone that normally controls blood glucose levels). These are meal dependent medicines (may lead to hypoglycemia if meals are delayed or skipped) and should be taken as prescribed with the balance in diet.

This brings us to answer a question, ***is there any diabetic diet?*** There is no diet called as diabetic diet. The plan advised should be ***Nutritionally adequate*** i.e. it should meet with all the requirements of nutrients of the individual; ***Individualized*** i.e. we cannot have one plan for suiting and meeting every patient's requirement and targets; ***Flexible*** i.e. the plan should give options in diet (during travel or eat out or socializing) and ensure that the patient gets choices and variety maintaining his/her requirements for achieving their glycemic goal.

Key steps for an ideal diet plan

Following steps may help constructing a diet plan:

- **Assess the patients medical history, BMI, physical activity and diet history**

  Medical history means "A list of a person's previous illnesses, present conditions, symptoms, medicines, and health risk factors."

  BMI is a measure of the relative body fatness to evaluate risk factors associated with obesity. It is based on weight (in kg) with minimal clothing and height (in m^2) without shoes.

Grade	BMI (kg/m^2)
Under weight	< 18.5
Not obese	18.5-22.9
Grade 1	23-24.9
Grade 2	25-29.9
Grade 3	>= 30

  Physical activity can be classified in various forms as sedentary, moderate, active, bed ridden.

  Diet history is a method of dietary assessment in which subjects are asked to recall their food consumption over a specific period of time.

  Assessment = Medical History + Physical Activity Level + Diet History

  Nutrition assessment is used to determine what the individual with diabetes is able and willing to do

- **Determine calorie requirement**

Obese	20 Kcal/kg
Sedentary, inactive (men/women) Between 35yrs-55yrs	22-25 Kcal/kg
Sedentary (men/women) 55 yrs and above	28 Kcal/kg
(sedentary men/active women) Active (men/women)	30 Kcal/kg
Thin/Very active, Men	40 Kcal/kg

Points to Remember: Calories and protein prescribed should be based on present weight, weight gain/loss if required, growth and development.

Strategies may be aimed at improving food selection (e.g. reducing fats and saturated fats), spreading meals throughout the day, and advise regular exercise.

- **Determine dietary distribution of proximal principles CHO, Protein, Fat.**

  The distribution of macro nutrients is based on patient's current eating pattern but with a focus on dietary norms to be applied.

Quick Guide on T2DM Diet Major/Macro Nutrients

CHO		*Protein*		*Fats*	
Simple Easily absorbed in blood	*Complex Gradual absorption in blood*	*Class 1 Good quality*	*Class 2 Moderate quality*	*Visible Added while cooking*	*Invisible Present before cooking*
Sugar	Roti	Toned milk	All Dals	Refined Oil	Fish
Jam	Dalia	Egg white	Cereals	(all kinds)	Chicken
Honey	Oats	Paneer		Desi ghee	Mutton
Mithai	Whole	Curds		Processed	Eggs
Restricted					
Biscuit	wheat	Fish		Cheese	Milk
Soft drinks	Bread	Chicken		Dalda	Nuts
Fruit juice	Raw fruits	Soybean		Margarine	Dals
White Bread	Vegetables	*Daily protein = 1 g/kg*		Cream/	Cereals
Plain Rice		*present wt If nephropathy*		Malai	
Poha	*Moderate*	*= 0.8-1.0g/kg* If obese*		*Daily visible fat intake-*	
Suji	*amounts*	*= 1g/kg ideals body wt*		*3tsp-5tsp/day**	
Idli		*50% daily protein from*		** There could be individual*	
Dosa		*Class-1 sources*		*variation*	
50 per cent total calories		*If veg pt, may recommend;*			
from complex carbs		*Dals + Roti/Rice*			
		Milk(paneer/curds) + Rice/			
		Roti			

- **Formulation of meal plan.**
  After assessment and diet history it is the meal plan that needs to be planned as per the individual.
- **Distribution of carbohydrates and calories in relation to physical activity, oral hypoglycemic agents throughout the day.**

***Sweetners*:** Sweeteners are ingredients that add sweetness of foods like soft drinks, desserts, candies, pastries. There are 2 categories of sweetners.

a. Nutritive sweeteners—which have calories
b. Non-Nutritive sweeteners—w/o calories

Nutritive Sweetners

Sugar Name	*Description*
Sucrose	This form of carbohydrate is found in table sugar, raw sugar, cane sugar, powdered sugar and brown sugar. Sucrose is 50 per cent glucose and 50 per cent fructose.
Dextrose	Another name for glucose.
Honey	Honey is 35 per cent glucose and 40 per cent fructose, a close relative to Honey sucrose.
High Fructose Corn Syrup	Less expensive and sweeter than sucrose, it is primarily glucose. It is usually found in sodas and soft drinks.
Corn Syrup or Corn Sugar	Derived from cornstarch, this sugar is high in glucose.
Fructose	Fructose sweetner, fruit sugar. Because fructose is sweeter than sucrose, less can be used in recipes.
Maltose	Found in malt, beer, this sugar is formed from 2 glucose molecules. It is potent and adds quickly to the blood glucose pool.

Another form of nutritive sweetners include **Sugar alcohols.** They are:

- CHO with chemical structure that partially resembles both sugar and alcohol.
- Readily converts to sugar in liver, may also cause high TGs and wt gain.

- If taken in excess, may cause diarrhoea.
- 1g = 2 Kcal approx.

Sugar Name	*Description*
Sorbitol	Derived from glucose; this sweetener is 60 per cent as sweet as sucrose.
Xylitol	Derived from xylose, it is equal in sweetness to sucrose.
Isomalt	Derived from sucrose; it is about 60 per cent as sweet as sucrose.
Mannitol	Derived from mannose; it is about 70 per cent as sweet as sucrose.
Hydrogenated Starch Hydrolysates (HSH)	Derived from corn, wheat or potato starches. These sweeteners range from 40 per cent to 90 per centas sweet as sucrose.

***Non-nutritive Sweeteners*:** Non-nutritive sweeteners are added in very small amounts to foods for a significant sweetening effect. These sweeteners have been approved for use in a number of dietetic or reduced-calorie foods and beverages. While safety is a concern, only minute amounts are necessary.

Saccharin	Saccharin is about 300 times as sweet as sucrose. It has been in use since the late 1800s and is a popular tabletop sweetener. In the 1970's, its safety was questioned in the United States because of studies suggesting an increased risk of bladder cancer in male rats given very high levels of saccharin. Later, the research design was called into question and its conclusions refuted. It is now determined that up to 1 gram per day of saccharin poses no health risks to adults. While there is no evidence of harmful effects reported, recent studies show that saccharin does cross the placenta and may be of concern to some women during pregnancy.
Acesulfame K	Acesulfame Potassium (K) is 200 times as sweet as sucrose. It is heat stable so, unlike aspartame, it can be used in cooking. It is added to dry mixes for sugar free gelatins, puddings and beverages. It can also be used in baked goods. In Canada and Europe it is approved for soft drinks. There are no safety concerns raised about Acesulfame K. It has been deemed safe for all age groups.

Aspartame	Aspartame is 200 times sweeter than sucrose. It became available as a tabletop sweetener in the 1970s and is now added to thousands of foods. It is not stable in heat nor for long periods in liquid form. While the U.S. Food and Drug Administration stated that high heat or long storage times could decrease the quality of the food products, they concluded that this did not pose a health risk. The FDA has approved aspartame for use during pregnancy and lactation. The Center for Disease Control did state that some individuals might be unusually sensitive to aspartame. Anyone who experiences a reaction to aspartame is encouraged to document it and discuss it with his or her physician. Phenylalanine is a component of aspartame that should be avoided by individuals with a rare metabolic disorder called phenylketonuria (PKU). Phenylalanine does cross the placenta and has been a concern in producing PKU in offspring. However, even at high levels of intake placental transport of this substances does not appear to be clinically harmful.
Sucralose	Sucralose is a non-caloric sweetener that is made from sugar. It was approved in April of 1998 for use as a table top sweetener. It is now used to sweeten products in more than 30 countries. Sucralose is 600 times sweeter than sugar and it is heat-stable, which means it can be used for baked goods. Sucralose has no effect on blood sugar, offers no calories and is deemed safe for use with all populations, including pregnant and lactating women as well as children.

Sweetners	**ADI (mg/kg body wt)**
ACESULFAME K	15 mg/kg body wt./day
(Sunette, Sweet One)	
ASPARTAME	50 mg/kg body wt./day
(Equal, Sugar free, Natra Sweet)	
SACCHARIN	5 mg/kg body wt./day
SUCRALOSE	15 mg/kg body wt./day
(Splenda, Zero, Elata)	

Note: ADI—Acceptable dietary intake

***Micronutrients*:** When dietary intake is adequate, there is generally no need for additional vitamin and mineral supplementation for the majority of people with diabetes. Micronutrient should be supplemented/modified on indication. Restircted diets usually require supplementation.

***Hypoglycemia*:** is low blood sugar. When blood sugars fall below <70mg/dl, it is diagnosed as hypoglycemia in a diabetes patient.

- An issue for individuals on Insulin secretagogues.
- Changes in food intake, physical activity, medication(s) except JANUVIA can contribute to the development of hypoglycemia.
- Glucose is the preferred treatment for hypoglycemia,
- Ingestion of 15-20 g of glucose is effective.

***Hypertension*:** A reduction in sodium intake lowers BP. Goal should be to reduce Na intake to 2,400 mg Na = 1tsp/day (levelled). Modest amount of weight loss beneficially affects BP.

***Diabetes Nephropathy*:** Nephropathy means kidney disease or damage. Diabetic nephropathy is damage to your kidneys caused by diabetes. In severe cases it can lead to kidney failure. But not everyone with diabetes has kidney damage.

The kidneys have many tiny blood vessels that filter waste (sodium, potassium and phosphorus) and water from your blood. High blood sugar from diabetes can destroy these blood vessels. Over time, the kidney isn't able to do its job as well. Later it may stop working completely. This is called kidney failure.

Dietary Management of diabetes nephropathy

- Work with your doctor to keep your blood pressure in the target range.
- Keep your heart healthy by eating a low-fat diet and exercising regularly.
- What how much protein you eat. Eating too much is hard on your kidneys. Reduction of dietary protein of 0.8-1.0g/

kg/day and for people with micro albuminuria a reduction to 0.8 g/kg/day.

- Keep a check on your salt intake and over all sodium in the diet.
- Don't smoke or use other tobacco products.

Fibre in diet helps in

1. Controlling diabetes by preventing excessive rise in blood glucose after meals.
2. Helps in decreasing blood cholesterol and triglycerides so less chances of getting heart attack.
3. Helps in reducing weight: Becomes bulky and gives feeling of fullness thereby lowers appetite and calorie intake.

How Much Calories are Needed

If you are over weight	20 cal/kg/day
If you are ideal weight	30 cal/kg/day
If you are under weight	40 cal/kg/day

Weight is calculated as per the height and body frame tables.

The basic principles behind creating high quality Health Foods are:

1. Add alteast 2% dietary fibres to all preparations.
2. Use only those ingredients which are rich in fibres, vitamins, minerals and flavonoids, such as, whole grains, vegetables/fruits.
3. Use ingredients which are rich in EFAs, sterols and antioxidant Vitamin E, like wheat germs, soyabean, sesame and almond/apricot.
4. Keep density of foods light and make these balanced, i.e. proper ratio of proteins, carbohydrates, fibres and fats.

Which Sweeteners

Not Honey As It Equates With Sugar

Non-nutritive sweetners, e.g., Saccharine, Aspartame are suitable especially if weight is a problem.

Avoid Sorbitol and Fructose.

Ghee or Refined Vegetable Oil

There has been a sudden and sharp rise in prevalence of many diseases specially heart disease, kidney disease and Diabetes. It is because, we have deviated from our traditional low fat diet and have adopted fast food culture.

This fast, fatty, fried, refined, processed and preserved food has ill-balanced high fat content. It is deficit in an important essential fatty acid (n:3fat) which is found in green leafy vegetables, mustard oil and seeds, fish oil, flax seed, and *methy*. This type of food contains n:6 fatty acids and high content of unsaturated fats.

People have been using ghee, butter and milk and yet they were having good health. Since the case of these vegetable redefined oils, there has been sharp increase in use of diabetes and heart diseases. Intake of storage fat and refined vegetable oils lead to weight gain and obesity. These adverse effect can be attributed to high content of Polyunsaturated n:6 fat contained in these animal fats and vegetable oils. Cholesterol in ghee and milk is limited in quantity. Indians consuming typical Indian diet do not get even the half the required quantity of cholesterol. One can use 2-3 teaspoon full of Ghee per person per day or 1/2 kg per month. Don't fry the items in Ghee. In India we have used these for centuries without any harm. The reason was people were using ghee, milk or butter and were doing regular exercise. Life was not sedentary as it is today. You can use Desi Ghee, milk and butter but should do regular exercise for at lease 30 minutes a day.

Dietitian

Every Diabetic should consult Dietitian who is expert in food and nutrition. Dietitian can help you to find out your food needs based on your weight, lifestyle and the type of treatment you are taking.

Diabetes and High Blood Pressure

People with Diabetes are more likely to have high blood pressure than non-diabetics. High blood pressure is a Risk factor for having a heart attack, or stroke and may cause or worsen kidney disease and retinopathy (eye disease).

Blood pressure is the force of your blood as it travels through your blood vessels. The higher your blood pressure, the more force on your blood vessels and this can weaken and damage blood vessels and finally damages organs and nerves.

Symptoms

High Blood Pressure (Hypertension) leads to

- Weakness, Headache,
- Fatigue, Tiredness
- Irritability

On each visit to your doctor you must get your blood pressure checked.

It is reported as systolic and diastolic Blood pressure. Systolic Blood Pressure is the force of your blood when your heart contracts. Diastolic pressure is the force of your blood when heart relaxes.

Blood pressure is written as 130/80 mm of Hg

120 is Systolic Blood pressure. 80 is Diastolic Pressure. It is measured as mm of Hg.

Target Blood Pressure

In adults with Diabetes

* Normal less than 120/80 mm of Hg

* Mild hypertension 130/80 to 140/90
* Moderate Hypertension 140/90 to 160/100
* Severe Hypertension 160/100 and above

Many people still think Blood pressure for different age groups is different. They calculate Blood Pressure as age +100.

This is wrong. For all adults blood pressure should be less than 130/80.

In patients with Type I Diabetes, High Blood Pressure is often caused by underlying diabetic kidney disease.

In Type II Diabetic patients it is present in more than 50 per cent of cases at the time of diagnosis, as a part of diabetic metabolic disorder.

Aggressive blood pressure control reduces the vascular complications of diabetes.

To Lower Your Blood Pressure

1. *Reduce excess weight* :- Loosing few kg weight can bring your blood pressure to normal. Best way to lose weight is to follow a weight-loss diet and an exercise programme.

2. *Stop Smoking* :- Smoking plays important role in causing blood pressure by damaging blood vessels. Stopping smoking can help not only in lowering the risk of Hypertension related death but also reduces the number of blood pressure controlling medicines.

3. *Reduce Alcohol Intake*:- More than 60ml intake of alcohol everyday may cause high blood pressure. 30ml alcohol twice or three times a week may be taken if one cannot live without it.

4. *Eat less salt* :- Reducing the amount of salt may be enough to lower your blood pressure.

5. *Reduce stress* :- Stress may increase your blood pressure. During stress blood vessels constrict and Heart has to work hard.

If blood pressure does not come down with these measures then your doctor may put you on drugs to lower your blood pressure.

How to Improve Your Blood fat Levels

* Control Your Blood Sugar Levels.
* If you are over-weight, then lose few kilograms. Losing weight raises your good H.D.L. Cholesterol.
* More fat you eat, the more V.L.D.L. the liver makes More V.L.D.L. Means Bad L.D.L. Cholesterol.
* Replace saturated fats (Desi Ghee and Butter) with unsaturated fats (Vegetable oils). Saturated fats raise your L.D.L. and unsaturated fats lower them.
* Avoid foods which have high Cholesterol.
* Eat foods high in fiber. Beans, peas, fresh fruits are rich in fiber.
* Aerobic exercises such as brisk walk, jogging, and swimming, raise your good H.D.L. Cholesterol.
* Smoking lowers good H.D.L. Cholesterol. So quit or cut down.

Have your Lipid profile tested at least once a year.

Disadvantages of Over Cooking

Lately lot of attention has been diverted to the harmful effects of various methods of cooking. *It was earlier felt that over cooking kills bacteria and makes the food sterile and safe for eating and therefore a lot of people had erred on the side of over cooking rather than under cooking. It certainly helps in killing bacteria but recent research has shown a lot of harmful effects of over cooking.*

1. It has been shown that by *over cooking or exposing food to high temperature for long periods of time, sugars get converted into Advanced Glycation End products (AGE's) which irritate the cells of the body and release certain triggers of inflammation like C Reactive Protein.* These advanced glycation end products are associated with disorders *commonly found* in adults as they get older *like hypertension* (High Blood Pressure), *diabetes, stroke, dementia, vision problems, skin changes,* nervous system and skin disorders. *AGE's* are produced more with *animal derived products,* for example *cheese, bacon and sausages* on exposure to *high temperature.* If one adds water, specially the use of *steaming,* it delays *this* reaction leading to the *production of AGE's* and is therefore beneficial. *Dry high temperature* is the worst *culprit* in this matter.

2. It has been shown that exposure of starch rich food (*such as fried potatoes, potato chips, some* types of *breakfast cereals and baked food*) *to high* temperature *leads to production* of *a substance* called "*Acrylamide*" which is a *cancer producing* substance and has been associated with some forms of cancer. *Frying, baking,* roasting and

grilling for long periods are *most* likely to reach these *temperatures* and may be *harmful*. Even use of *pasteurised food especially* milk may be harmful.

3. Also certain vitamins, specially *water soluble Vitamins B, C and E,* are *dramatically unstable* and they get *destroyed on exposure to* high temperature.

4. Over cooking also *reduces the carotene level* of the *food and therefore Vitamin A, which is very* important for proper vision and *for development* of retina, gets *depleted* in the food.

5. Repeated exposure to high temperature, specially *repeated frying of vegetables, Samosas and Pakoras in the same oil again and again,* leads to production of a special form *of fat called "Trans Fatty Acids", which are extremely dangerous as they deposit in the wall of the arteries leading to their clogging and blocking.* Depending on the area or the organ of the body where these trans fatty acids lodge *are the* effects *noticed.* For example if trans fatty acids get deposited in the arteries of the *heart, one can get heart attacks;* if in the arteries of *the brain,* one *gets stroke; in the eyes, it can lead to blindness*; in the *kidneys* to kidney *failure and in the legs* to *pain in the legs* on walking (*claudication*) and some *times even to gangrene ending ultimately with amputations.* These trans fatty acids are actually the atherogenic i.e. cholesterol depositing form of fat and are very *dangerous.*

6. Besides that over cooking leads to vegetables loosing their normal lustre so that they become dull and they also loose their delecate flavour and aroma of herbs which are very important for normal salivation and for digestion of food.

With so many disadvantages of *over cooking food, it* is *therefore, just appropriate to know what is the best* cooking *method for good health of the* whole family. For a healthy heart, we must *eat food prepared* by such a cooking method that there is minimum loss of *nutrients*. There are various methods recommended for cooking:

a. ***Boiling*** **:** The simplest method of cooking is boiling. It is the cooking of *food in a* rapidly boiling liquid *at a temperature* of 100°C. But the main disadvantages being loss of *nutrients,* colour and flavour.

b. **Simmering :** When foods are cooked in a pan with a well *fitting lid* at a temperature just below the boiling point of the liquid in which they are immersed (water—82-99°C), the process is known as simmering. Advantage of this method is that loss of *nutrients* is less.

c. **Steaming :** To *retain the nutritive value of food, steaming is a very good method.* Steaming is the process of *cooking food in steam from a boiling* liquid, *usually water.* There is less loss of nutrients as there is no leaching *and* cooking time is less. Colour and flavour of vegetables is retained *in this* method.

d. **Pressure Cooking :** In pressure cooking, escaping steam is trapped and kept under pressure so that the temperature of the boiling water and steam can be raised *above 100°C* and reduce the cooking time. There is loss *of flavour* and colour.

e. **Grilling :** Cooking is done *under a source* of radient heat. There *is less loss of nutrients* and improved *flavour of food,* but one can do over cooking unless *one is* careful.

f. **Roasting :** When food is cooked uncovered on *heated metal* or frying *pan the method is known* as *roasting.* There is loss of nutrients *like* amino acids when the food becomes brown.

g. **Sautéing :** This method involves cooking in just enough of oil to cover the base of pan (greasing the pan). The heat is transformed to food mainly by conduction.

In general, *Frying, Grilling and Microwave cooking for long periods lead to very high temperatures as compared to boiling and steaming*. The ideal method of cooking, which is recommended, is *a combination of steaming and sautéing.*

The advantages which are seen by using these methods are:

a. Nutritive value of food is maintained because there is no leaching and cooking time is less.
b. Easily digestible and not much fat is added.
c. Texture of food is better, light and fluffy.
d. Flavour of sauted and steamed food is good.
e. It is ideal for those with poor digestion.

Lifestyle

The basic concept of a healthy lifestyle is:

* Maintain your body weight according to your age and height by controlling calories intake.
* Regular exercise is the only key to keep Blood Sugar and Blood Pressure under control only with weight.
* Discard "junk foods" which are loaded with saturated fats and/or sugar (all deep fried food, chocolates, ice creams, artificial drinks).
* Discard alcohol and tobacco and cut down on tea/coffee.
* Adopt natural foods, vegetables, fruits, cereals, legumes and nuts and only scientifically processed health foods (always look for the labels).
* Cut down the size of your meals and increase the frequency.
* Do not restrict your diet to a few selected food — *variety is the key.*

Exercise

Importance of Exercise is mentioned in all ancient books and Ayurveda. Physicians like Shushrata and Charak have mentioned the benefits of exercise especially in Diabetic patients.

They have advised horse riding, long brisk walks and wrestling for obese diabetic patients. Participation in above sports and all other sports reduces blood sugar levels.

Every person should consult his physician before joining any exercise programme. Exercise programme is different for each individual and it depends upon many factors like age of patient and associated high blood pressure and other problems. If Physician advises you to undergo some investigations like E.C.G. etc., then you must undergo these investigations.

Exercise should be performed five days in a week, 40-45 minutes each day. One should start exercise slowly and increase it gradually.

Certain points to remember—

* Exercise should be performed on an empty stomach.
* One should wear loose and comfortable clothes (dress).
* One should avoid lifting of heavy weights.
* Avoid exercise in extreme hot or cold climate.

Precautions for Exercise

Before starting an exercise programme, certain factors to be kept in mind:

* If one is over 40 years of age.
* If one has never participated in strenuous physical activity since younger days.
* If one is over weight.
* If one is a heavy smoker.
* If one has high blood pressure or is suffering from angina.

Evaluation by a physician and complete health checkup including E.C.G. are essential prior to undertaking any exercise programme for the above mentioned people. Persons with diabetic foot and peripheral vascular disease, should avoid running, and choose cycling or swimming for exercise.

In the presence of retinal involvement (retinopathy), diabetics should avoid exercise associated with increased abdominal pressure or sudden acceleration or trauma to head and lifting of weight. In the presence of hypertension, avoid heavy weight lifting and choose exercise that involve lower limbs, i.e.walking.

One should observe the following precautions during exercise:

* Start with warm up exercises.
* One should not exercise straight after eating.
* Exercise should not be done under extremes of temperature.
* It is unwise to exercise if one has some infection or common cold.
* One should not participate in competitive programmes (game, matches, etc.) unless fully trained or has been practising earlier in the field.
* If chest pain occurs during exercise, one should stop exercise immediately and consult a doctor.
* If one is restarting exercise after a break of 2 weeks or so, one should start slowly.

Advantage of Exercise

Regular Exercise prevents risk factors for heart attack and high blood pressure.

* Fat and cholesterol levels fall with regular exercise.
* It gives you feeling of well being.
* Utilisation of calories helps to control weight.
* Reduces weight.
* Helps in controlling blood sugar.

Precautions before Exercise

If you have heart or joint problems or are very overweight or have never exercised much before, it is particularly important that you talk to your doctor. If you develop chest or leg pains during exercise it is important to stop exercising and tell your doctor.

Some Helpful Hints—

* Walk upstairs instead of taking a lift.
* Don't sit down when you are waiting for bus or train. But stroll about instead.
* Play more actively with your children or grandchildren.
* Take your dog for longer walks.
* Wear comfortable, well-fitting shoes and socks for exercising.
* Cool down at the end of the session by gradually decreasing your level of exercise over 5-10 minutes.

What Type? How to Achieve Target? What Precautions?

Aerobic exercises are ones that use your heart, lungs, arms, and legs. By working these parts of your body, you can improve your blood flow, reduce your risk of heart disease, and lower your blood pressure. You can also lower your LDL cholesterol (bad cholestrol) and triglycerides and raise your HDL cholesterol (the good cholestrol).

When you do aerobic exercises, you breathe harder and your heart beats faster. This builds your endurance and increases your energy. You may find that aerobic exercises help you sleep better, make you feel less stressed, balances your emotions, and improves your sense of well-being.

Aerobic exercise is not only good for your heart but is also good for your diabetes. Aerobic exercise makes your Insulin work harder and faster, reduces your body fat, and helps you lose weight. If you don't exercise already, your doctor may advise you to start.

What to do Before you Start

Check with your doctor before you start any exercise. Your doctor may want some tests to see how your heart, blood vessels, eyes, feet, and nerves are doing. Your blood pressure, blood fat levels, glycohemoglobin levels, and body fat might also be checked. Your doctor or nurse can tell you how to adjust your diabetes-care plan for exercise.

What Aerobic Exercises to do

Some exercises may make heart, eye, feet, or nerve problems worse. Your doctor may like to do some test to check your heart and blood vessels, before advising what kinds of exercises are safe for you to do. Pick from these exercises a few, you think, you might enjoy. Then learn the right way to do each exercise. Here are some examples of aerobic exercises:

* Aerobic classes
* Bicycling

* Dancing
* Jogging
* Jumping rope
* Rowing
* Running
* Skating (roller, ice, in-line)
* Skiing (downhill, cross-country)
* Stair climbing
* Swimming
* Walking

How Long and How Often to Exercise

If you are just starting to exercise after a long time of little or no activity, go for 5 minutes. Build up to short bouts of exercise that add up to at least 30 minutes a day. For example, you might try brisk walking or stair climbing for 10 minutes three times a day or for 15 minutes twice a day.

Exercising for less than 15 minutes a day is not likely to improve your health. Gradually build up to 20 to 60 minutes of continuous aerobic exercise three to five times a week. The 20 to 60 minutes of aerobic exercise does not include your warm-up and cooldown.

A warm-up will slowly raise your heart rate, warm your muscles, and help prevent injuries. A cooldown will lower your heart rate and slow your breathing. Warm up for 5 to 10 minutes before aerobic exercise, and cooldown for 5 to 10 minutes after aerobic exercise. As a warm-up or a cool down, you could gently stretch, walk, or slowly bicycle.

How Hard to Exercise

Your doctor, nurse, or exercise specialist can tell you how hard to exercise by giving you a number. The number is a percentage. It may be as low as 40 per cent or as high as 70 per cent. It is a percentage of your capacity for exercise (your maximum aerobic capacity). There are a few ways to figure out your maximum aerobic capacity. Here's one easy way.

Subtract your age from 220. The answer is your maximum heart rate. For example, if you are 40, your maximum heart rate is 180. To exercise at 60 per cent of your maximum aerobic capacity, keep your pulse at 108 beats per minute ($180 \times 60\% = 108$). A nurse can show you how to take your pulse.

When to Exercise

A good time to exercise is 1 to 3 hours after you finish a meal or snack. The food you have eaten will help keep your blood glucose level from falling too low.

Do not Exercise when

* Your blood glucose level is over 300mg/dl.
* Your insulin or diabetes pills are peaking.
* You have ketones in your urine.
* You have numbness, tingling, or pain in your feet or legs.
* You are short of breath.
* You are ill.
* You have a serious injury.
* You feel dizzy.
* You have pain/tightness in your chest, neck, shoulders, or jaw.
* You have blurred sight of blind spots.

Role of Yoga

There are various schools of thought and according to them various yogic exercises are good for controlling Blood Sugar levels. Some of the *ASANAS* are specially useful for controlling Diabetes.

Dangers of Exercise (Without medical supervision)

Before planning for Exercise one should consult Doctor to evaluate his cardiac (heart) status. If person is having underlying heart disease and he/she starts strenuous exercise it might precipitate fresh attack of angina or heart attack and may even cause death. In old age arthritis also restricts the movements of joints and can cause stiffness in joints.

Yoga has become popular all over world. System of Yoga was developed by great *yogis* thousands of years ago. It teaches discipline and keeps the body physically fit.

One can learn the art of yoga by regular practice. Initially it would be difficult to assume the correct posture but gradually one can learn. Before trying yoga; please consult your doctor.

Following yogic exercises are useful for diabetic patients. Although there are many asanas but I have selected a few which can be done easily without much difficulty.

1. Ardhnav Asana

It helps to activate functioning of gall bladder, kidneys and pancrease.

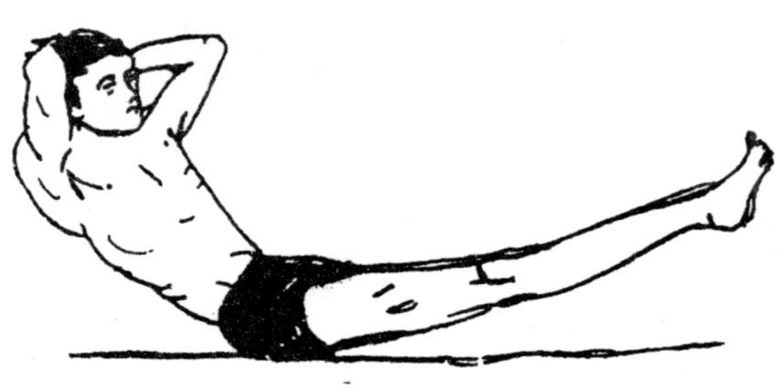

2. Dhanur Asana

It activates all glands of body specially Pancrease and helps in release of Insulin hormone.

3. Janusshirsh Asana

This asana helps in improving the functioning of Liver and Pancrease.

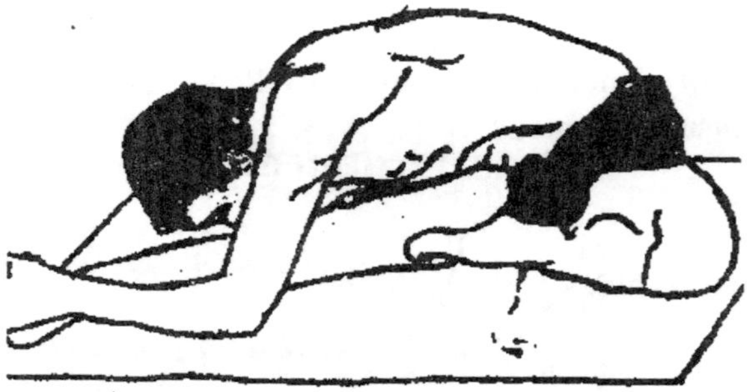

4. Ardhmatsyendra Asana

This asana is specially useful for diabetics and it stimulates the functioning of Pancrease gland.

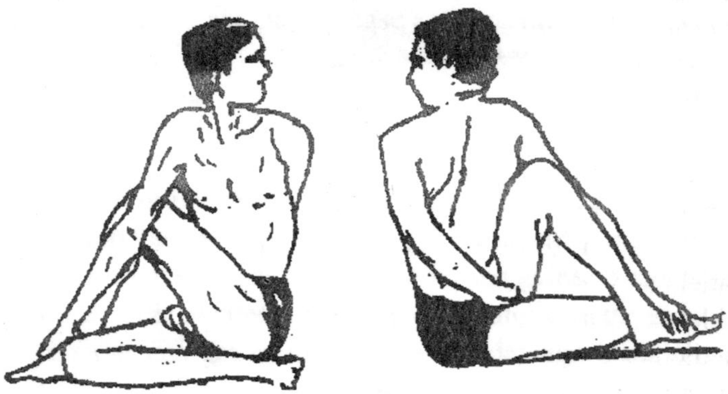

Precautions

* In persons who are having Retinal involvement (Eye involvement) strenuous exercise may cause Retinal detachment and sudden blindness.
* Take care of your food before and after exercise and inspect for any vesicles, cuts or any change in colour of nails.
* One should keep sugar with one-self as suddenly Blood Sugar may fall during exercise and timely intake of sugar will prevent hypoglycemia (low blood sugar).

Drug Treatment

Oral Hypoglycemic Agents (OHA) / Tablets

If by regular exercise and with proper food control Blood Sugar is not under control, then patient is advised to take medicines for lowering Blood Sugar.

Diabetes is chronic problem and one had to take medicines for a longer time, along with diet control and exercise.

If the Random blood sugar level is persistently above 250mg per cent in spite of good diet control and regular exercise your doctor will advise you to take medicines. These are tablets belonging to two different groups (i) Sulfonyl Urea and (ii) Bigunides.

All the medicines are given in low doses initially and patients are advised to take these medicines before meals or after meals—depending upon the medicine.

There are different indications for these medicines so each patient should follow doctor's advise and should not change these tablets as per the advise of other patients. One should avoid taking medicines along with alcohol as sometimes there can be severe adverse effects of it.

Main side effect of all these medicines is hypoglycemia, other side effect are itching all over body, nausea, vomiting, giddiness, distension of adomen, constipation or diarrhoea.

Use of pain-killers along with these drugs increases effects of these medicines.

Who are the persons who will need these tablets?

1. Persons with NIDDM or Maturity onset diabetes, i.e. above the age of 40 years.
2. Whose requirement for Insulin is less.
3. Whose diabetes is of short duration.

4. Use of these medicines along with Insulin, in adult patients.
5. Should not be given to children Type-I (IDDM) with Diabetes.

Points to Remember

* *All tablets are not alike.* In one person one tablet may be more effective while it may not be helpful to other. So don't change your medicines on other patients advise.
* For each patient different tablets are prescribed depending upon the weight, and nature of job. *So don't stop your tablets and change them without your Doctor's advice.*
* Don't take *tablets with alcohol.*
* If you have missed one dose don't take extra dose next time.
* Diabetic children should not be given tablets.
* Pregnant ladies should not be given tablets if they are diabetic.
* Tablets should be taken 1/2 an hour before breakfast and dinner.

Blood Glucose—Lowering Medications Oral Blood Glucose Lowering Medications Category: Sulfonylureas*

Action: To stimulate insulin secretion in the pancreatic β-cells (Can cause hypoglycemia)

Generic Name	*Trade Name*	*Common Dose*	*Usual Frequency*
glimepiride	Amaryl	1, 2, 4 mg Max to 8 mg daily	One to two times daily
glipizide	Glucotrol Glucotrol XL Glynase, (extended release)	2.5–5 mg Up to 40 mg daily; 20 mg with XL daily	One to two times daily (XL taken once daily)
glyburide	Diabeta Micronase Glynase PresTab	1.25–10 mg	One to two times daily
Gliclazide	Glizide Diamilrone	40, 80mg	One to two times daily

* Only second generation of sulfonylureas listed. First generation of these drugs are, generally, no longer in use.

Category: Meglinitinides

Action: To stimulate insulin secretaion in the pancreatic β-cells. However, these have a shorter action time than sulfonylureas and are designed to be taken prior to meals to lower postprandial glucose. (Can cause hypoglycemia.)

Generic Name	*Trade Name*	*Common Dose*	*Usual Frequency*
repaglinide	Novanorm Eurepa	0.5–1.0 mg Upto 16 mg daily	Before meals, three times daily. Omit if meal not eaten.
nateglinide	Starlix	60-120 mg Up to 360 mg daily	Before meals, three times daily. Omit if meal not eaten.

Category: Biguanides

Action: Suppress glucose production in the liver and decrease insulin resistance. Increase glucose uptake by the muscles. (do not cause hypoglycemia.)

Generic Name	*Trade Name*	*Common Dose*	*Usual Frequency*
metformin	Glucophage Glyciphage Glycomet-XR (extended release) Fortamet Riomet (liquid)	500-1,000 mg dose Up to 2,550 mg daily; max effective dose 2,000 mg daily	Two times a day. Slow titration suggested.

Category: Thiazolidinediones (TZDs)

Action: Decrease insulin resistance in adipose and muscle cells.

Generic Name	*Trade Name*	*Common Dose*	*Usual Frequency*
pioglitazone	Actos/Pioz	15-45 mg	Once a day
rosiglitazone	Avandia	2-8 mg	Two times a day

Category: Alpha-Glucosidase inhibitors

Action: Decrease carbohydrate absorption in the gastrointestinal tract.

Generic Name	*Trade Name*	*Common Dose*	*Usual Frequency*
acarbose	Glucobay	Initiate at 25 mg and raise to max of 100 mg	With first bite of food at main meals
miglitol	Glyset	Initiate at 25 mg and raise to max of 100 mg	With first bite of food at main meals

Category: Dipeptidyl peptidase-4 inhibitors (DPP-4) inhibitors

Action: Block the breakdown of glucagon-like peptide-1 (GLP-1) by blocking the effects of the enzyme dipeptidyl peptidase. This action helps to increase the synthesis and release of insulin from the pancreatic β-cells and decreases the release of glucagon from the pancreatic alpha cells in the presence of elevated blood glucose levels.

Generic Name	*Trade Name*	*Common Dose*	*Usual Frequency*
Sitagliptin	Januvia	100 mg	Once a day
Vildagliptin	Galvus	50mg	once/twice daily
Suxagliptin	Onglyza	5mg	one daily

Combination meds

There is an increasing array of combinations of the above medications available for use in treating type 2 diabetes. They can be beneficial for some people by reducing the number of medications taken. However, it is more difficult to adjust each medication because the combinations are only available in certain dosage levels. Several of the combination medications available are:

- Pioz-MF—metformin + pioglitazone

- Avandamet—rosiglitazone + metformin
- Avandaryl—rosiglitazone + glimepiride
- Pioglar-G—pioglitazone + glimepiride
- Glucovance—glyburide + metformin
- Janumet—metformin + sitagliptin
- Metaglip—glipizide + metformin
- Glucored—Metformin + Glibenclamide

Injectable Blood Glucose Lowering Medications

Category: Incretin mimetics

Actions: Mimic the action of glucagon-like peptide (GLP-1) to increase insulin synthesis and secretion in the presence of elevated blood glucose levels, improve first-phase insulin response and reduce glucagon concentration when blood glucose is elevated, slow gastric emptying to slow the rise of blood glucose post meal and promote satiety (resulting in a lowered total calorie intake due to reduced hunger).

Generic Name	*Trade Name*	*Common Dose*	*Usual Frequency*
exenatide	BYETTA	5-10 μg in a pen that delivers the specified do (either 5 or 10 μg)	Two times a day before morning and evening meals
enatide	VICTOZA		given one daily by pen

Category: Amylin analog

Action: To help replace amylin, a hormone normally co-secreted with insulin from the pancreatic β-cells, in people with type 1 and insulin-requiring type 2 diabetes who have diminished amylin secretion. Pramlintide, the synthetic form of amylin, slows the rise of blood glucose after meals by slowing gastric emptying, suppressing glucagon secretion and promoting satiety (resulting in a lowered total calorie intake due to reduced hunger).

Generic Name	*Trade Name*	*Common Dose*	*Usual Frequency*
pramlintide acetate	SYMLIN	15 to 60 µg for type 1 Up to 120 µg for type 2	Taken before meals containing 30 g carbohydrate or 250 calories.

Switch over to Insulin

If with diet control, exercise and full dosage of these medicines, Blood Sugar is not under control, i.e. above 200mg% then your Doctor will advise you to use Insulin injections to control diabetes.

> 10-15 years after using OHA tablets the efficacy of these medicines is decreased this is called secondary failure to these agents and such patients are also advised to take Insulin.

WHAT YOU SHOULD KNOW ABOUT TABLETS

When Oral Hypoglycemic Agents (OHA) Tablets Fail

"Oral hypoglycemic agents have, in most patients, only a temporary effect." And many times after taking these tablets for many years there is no effect.

Primary Failure

Approximately 30 per cent of Type II diabetics fail to respond to oral hypoglycemic agents singly or in combinations.

Secondary Failure

"About 5 to 10 per cent of patients per year who respond initially to a sulfonylurea tablets, e.g. Daonil, Glynase, Euglucon etc., become secondary failures, as defined by unacceptable levels of hyperglycemia." They will not respond to these medicines and their Blood Sugar would remain high.

Changing Oral Agents does not improve Secondary Failure

"Patients who fail maximal doses first generation sulfonylurea should not be expected to respond to second-generation oral agent and should be changed to Insulin." One should avoid changing tablets from one brand to other as there will not be of any benefit at this stage.

Insulin

Before the invention of Insulin it was difficult for Diabetic patients to survive beyond the age of 20 years. Now there are patients who are using Insulin from the last 30 to 40 years and leading normal life.

Insulin was invented in 1926 by Dr. Fredrik Banting and Dr. Charles Best, since then many changes have taken place in the structure and potency. Today various types of Insulin are available for diabetic patients.

Insulin is hormone secreted by the pancrease.

There are three sources of *Insulin Pork Insulin— Porcine Insulin, Bovine Insulin, Human Insulin.*

Now-a-days purified Insulin are also available.

Insulin are of two types

* Plane—colourless—Short Acting
* NPH or Lente—Milky colour—long Acting

Which patients need Insulin:

1. All patients of IDDM or Type I Diabetes (Insulin Dependent Diabetes patients).
2. Patients of NIDDM or Type II Diabetes (Non-Insulin Dependent Diabetes) who develop secondary drug failure to oral agents. In all such cases insulin is given for short period.
3. Pregnant diabetic women.
4. Diabetic patients who are undergoing major surgery like Coronary By-Pass Surgery, or Eye Surgery or other major surgery.
5. Patients who develop Kidney failure.

Category: Insulin

Action: Lowers blood glucose levels by stimulating peripheral glucose uptake by the skeletal muscle and fat and by inhibiting helpatic glucose production. (Can cause hypoglycemia.)

Type of Insulin	*Generic Name*	*Trade Name*	*Onset of Action*	*Peak of Action*	*Duration of Action*
Rapid-acting	lispro aspart glulisine	Humalog Novolog Apridra	5-15 minutes	1-2 hours	≤5 hours
Short-acting	regular, human	Humulin R Novolin R Relion	30-60 minutes	2-4 hours	6-10 hours
Inter-mediate	NPH, human	Humulin N Novolin N ReliOn	2-4 hours	4-10 hours	10-16 hours
Long-acting	glargine detemir	Lantus Levemir	1-2 hours	Flat	20-24 hours

Notes on Insulin

1. Insulin action can vary from person to person. The onset, peak, and duration of action provided above are what is generally seen and reported in the literature.
2. Insulin is available in premixed combinations. These combinations are available as vials of insulin or insulin pens. The combinations available today are generally combinations of NPH and regular insulin or a combination of insulin analogs. Common combinations are 70/30, 75/25, and 50/50 with the longer-acting component providing the larger amount.
3. Insulin is generally given in combinations, either through the use of two insulins injected individually, i.e., a long-acting insulin once or twice a day with a rapid-acting insulin at mealtimes, or a premixed insulin provided twice a day.

Even with Insulin injection one should follow strict diet control and regular Exercise Schedule.

Some Insulins are short acting, their effect starts immediately so one should take along with food. Other types of Insulins are intermediate or long acting, their action starts within 2-4 hours and lasts from 12 to 18 hours.

Types of Insulin available in India

Insulin injections are made as 40 units or/100units/ml depending upon the type of Insulin.

One should be careful while filling the syringe regarding the dose of Insulin and should consult Physician about adjusting the dose.

Insulin syringes are made up of plastic material one can use the same syringe 3 to 4 times. Insulin syringes can be kept in refrigerator after using it.

Your Doctor will advise you to take one injection or two injections or more depending upon the type of Diabetes and other associated conditions.

Oral drugs are also given along with Insulin in some cases for better control of Diabetes and weight.

Complications of Insulin Injections

1. Hypoglycemia (Low Blood Sugar).
2. Atrophy or abcess at the site of injection.
3. Itching at the site of injection.

These complications can be avoided by proper dosage of Insulin. Taking Insulin injections along with food and changing the site of injection frequently.

General Guidelines on Insulin Use

Insulin is mainstay of treatment in approximately 1/3rd of patients of diabetes. However, unless the patient is equipped with the knowledge and know how, the desired results cannot be obtained. Hence, the patient's education in various aspects of diabetes and its control is vital.

Storage

Insulin is ideally stored in a refrigerator at 2°-8°C. Insulin should not be kept in the freezer or exposed to extremes of temperature. The commercially available insulin can be kept at room temperatures for 6 to 8 weeks. Insulin vials after expiry date should never be used.

Strength

Insulin are available in 40 IU/ml or 100 IU/ml strengths. It is essential to use the appropriate syringe for them.

Insulin Injection Technique

It is advisable to gently shake the suspension before use. The vial can be rolled gently upside down and sideways between the hands to ensure uniform suspension. Then vial is turned upside down and air is injected by syringe. The amount of air injected should be equivalent to the units of insulin to be withdrawn.

The Insulin vials which require mixing are usually of Plain/ Regular (clear vial) and Lente/NPH (cloudy vial). For mixing insulins first clean the rubber stopper of each bottle with spirit

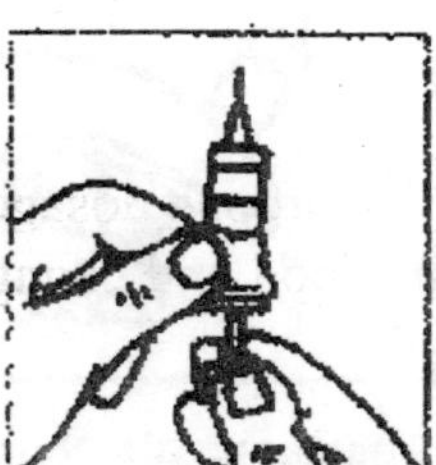

Draw air into the syringe in an amount corresponding to the prescribed dose of cloudy insulin.

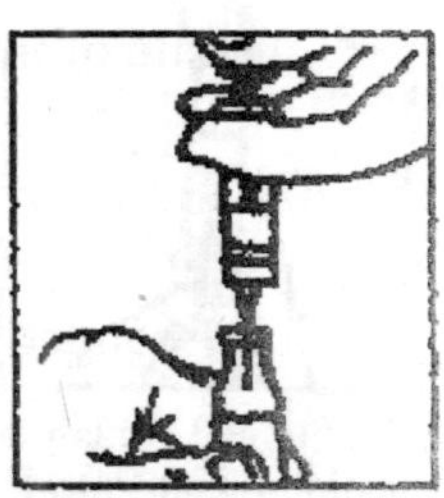

Inject the air into the vial containing the cloudy insulin—but do not draw up insulin!

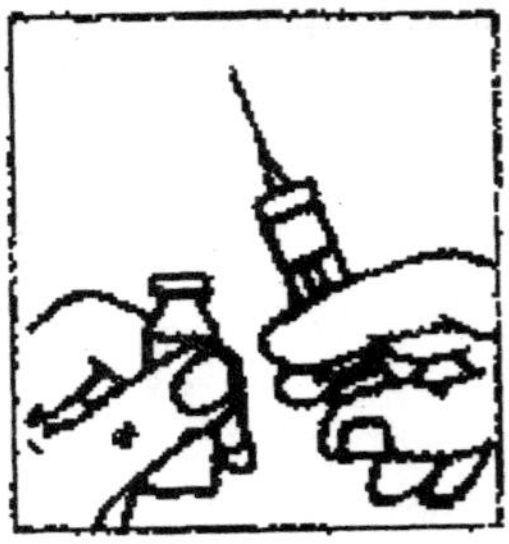

Pull out the needle and put the vial aside.

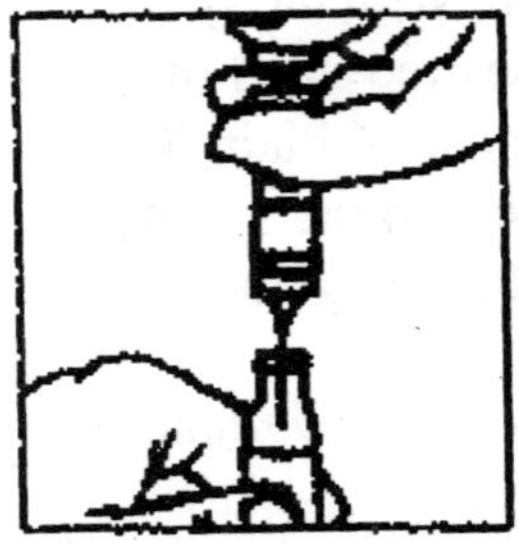

Draw air into the syringe in an amount corresponding to the prescribed dose of clear insulin and inject the air into the vial containing clear insulin.

Invert the vial and draw up clear insulin—a little more than prescribed.

Hold the vial vertically at eye level Inject the excess amount of insulin, together with any air bubbles, back into the vial. Pull out the needle

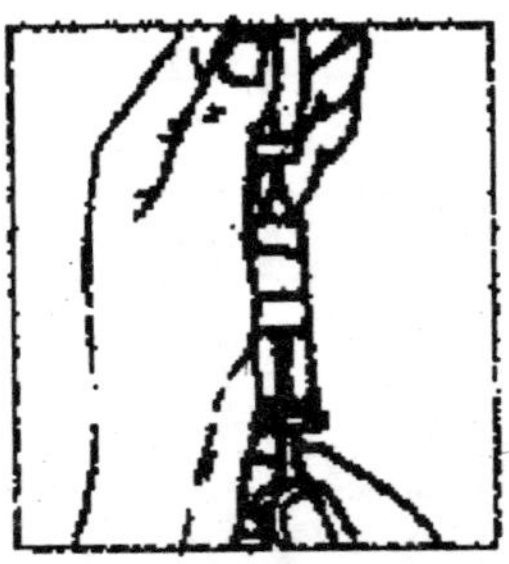

Now take the vial containing cloudy insulin and air. Insert the needle and draw up the accurate amount of insulin prescribed.

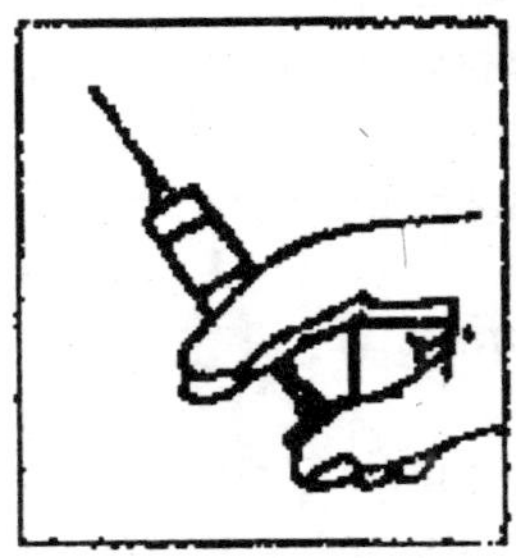

Pull out the needle. Now, the mixture is ready for use.

swab. With the syringe, draw the volume of air equivalent to level of desired units of Lente (cloudy) Insulin, later repeat the same for dose of Plain/Regular Insulin (clear). Ensure that there is not bubble in the syringe, (if present gently tap the syringe, to push the bubble to the top and then force it in the bottle).

Injection Technique

Clean the site selected (avoid spirit/alcohol swab) then skin is gently pinched between the thumb and forefinger, hold the syringe with the other hand like a pencil and needle is pushed through the skin, plunger is pushed and then the needle is withdrawn.

Site Selection and Rotation

Insulin should be injected into subcutaneous tissue, in any of the following areas: upper and outer area of arms, front and side areas of thigh, the buttocks, just above the waist, on the back, abdomen except the areas around the umblicus and at the waistline. The accidental intramuscular injection is painful and can cause tissue scaring. Massage or exercise of the area where injection is given, can alter the absorption of insulin so they should be avoided. Rotation of the side is important to avoid problems which could occur due to repeated injections at the same site. Rotation of the injection site should be about 1-½" length apart within the same area. If one feels lumps, or shallow depressions or feels pain or observes change of colour of the skin at the injection site, it is better to avoid that area till that condition disappears and also you should consult the doctor.

Timing

Insulin should be injected 30 to 45 minutes before the meals so that its onset of action corresponds to the rise in Blood Sugar that occurs with the meals.

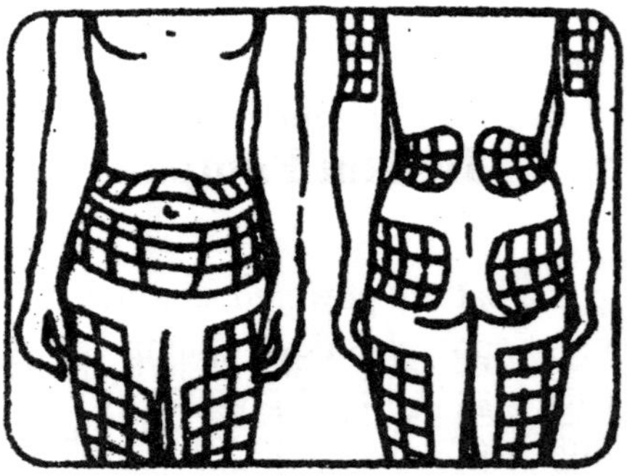

Site Selection and Rotation

Insulin and Exercise

Exercise can be associated with hypoglycemia in patients on insulin. Patient should make necessary adjustments in their meal plans or insulin regimen on the days of exercise in consultation with their doctor.

Insulin and Illness

Illness can disrupt diabetic control. However, the problems can be minimised, if the patients follows basic guidelines:

1. Do not stop the insulin injection,
2. Continue testing the Blood Sugar, urine sugar and ketones,
3. Adapt your eating patterns to more easily tolerated foods,
4. Food should be taken frequently after short intervals.

If the above simple precautions are observed by the patients who use insulin, many of their day to day problems can be avoided.

Pancrease Transplantation

Here pancrease gland of other person is transplanted into Diabetic patients. But there are many problems like availability of donor and rejection of graft by body.

Insulin Pumps

An insulin pump is a battery-powered, computerized device about the size of a deck of cards. Inside the pump is a syringe of short-acting insulin with a gear-driven plunger. A thin tube, 21 to 43 inches long, is attached to the pump. At the other end of the tube is a needle or catheter. You insert the needle or catheter under your skin, usually in your abdomen or thigh. Insulin is delivered through the tube and needle or catheter into your body.

You programme the pump. You tell it how much insulin you want and when you want it. You tell the pump to give you tiny amounts of short-acting insulin continuously throughout the day and night, just the way a normal pancrease would. Then you tell the pump to give you extra insulin just before you eat.

Your wear an insulin pump pretty much all the time, either inside or outside your clothes. A pump may be water-proof or come with a water-proof case for showers and swimming.

You can, of course, take the pump off. If you'll have the pump off for more than 1 hour, you may need a short of short-acting insulin. Check your blood glucose to be sure. Yes, you still need to test your blood glucose. At least four tests a day are recommended.

What the Pump can do for You

Get your blood glucose level closer to normal. This is called tight control. If your insulin shots have not controlled your blood glucose levels, in insulin pump might work better for you.

Smooth out blood glucose swings. If you have frequent blood glucose swings, the insulin pump can help smooth them out.

Take care of the night-time lows and the morning highs. Your body need less insulin at night than at dawn. If you try to lower the dose of your evening insulin shot to avoid low blood glucose at night, you won't enough insulin in the morning. Then you'll have high blood glucose when you wake up.

With an insulin pump, you can programme it to give you less insulin at night and more insulin before dawn. That way you avoid night-time low blood glucose and morning high blood glucose.

Be Aware

Ketoacidosis. When your body has too little or no insulin, you risk getting ketoacidosis. Ketoacidosis is a dangerous buildup of ketones in your blood.

If the tube to your insulin pumps gets blocked or twisted or the needle comes out, you won't be getting insulin, and you may not know it. (Pumps do have alarms that signal when the tube is blocked, the insulin is low, or the battery is low. But they don't signal when the needle has come out.)

Ketones can start to build up in 1 hour. Ketoacidosis can develop in as little as 6 hours. Your best protection is to check your blood glucose levels often. If your blood glucose level is over 250mg/dl, check your urine for ketones.

Infection. The place where the needle or catheter enters your body may become infected. To lessen your chances of infection, clean the area before you insert the needle or catheter, change sites within the area every 48 hours (See Insulin Shots), and use an antibiotic ointment and protective cover.

Skin allergy. You may have an allergic reaction around the needle or catheter site. Try non-allergenic tape or Teflon catheters.

Costs and Insurance

Pumps cost between Rs. 1 lakh to Rs. 2 lakh. Supplies for a month, including blood glucose monitoring strips, cost about Rs. 4000 to Rs. 5000.

If you think you may want a pump, talk to your doctor. Learning how to use a pump can take some time. Your doctor may want you to be in the hospital for a few days when you first get a pump so that you can learn all about how to use it.

Spontaneous Hypoglycaemia

Some people have a tendency to develop low blood sugar levels which can cause extreme weakness. In a normal person, fasting blood sugar levels are 70 to 100mg/100ml and 2 hours after food, blood sugar levels are between 100 to 140mg/100ml.

Some of these persons get up in the morning with headache and weakness which gets better with tea. Two hours after breakfast, they again get the feeling of *Ghabrahat*, palpitation, sweating and restlessness and these symptoms persist till the person eats something. These symptoms are due to low blood glucose—medical term is hypoglycemia. Blood sugar levels are usually less than 60mg/100ml.

Many people may be suffering from this condition but they are rarely diagnosed. Most of the time these patients are diagnosed having heart problems and referred to cardiologist or referred to psychiatrist for the treatment of depressions or anxiety.

If the blood sugar is tested during these episodes, it would be below the normal range, i.e. usually less then 60mg/100ml.

Large number of otherwise normal people occasionally become pale, weak, sweaty (sweating) before meals and such people report benefit from advice to take regular snacks between meals. True hypoglycemia may develop after food in the presence of alcohol which stimulates 'B' cells of pancreas gland to produce exaggerated response to carbohydrates. Persons who consume alchoholic beverages like Beer or other alcoholic drink during lunch time are potentially at risk of developing hypoglycaemia.

The symptoms people have, when they are having low blood sugar, are due to two things. First, the Brain itself cannot work properly when the blood glucose fall below 55 mg/100 ml and secondly, the body reacts to low blood glucose by producing hormones (mainly adrenalin) which increases blood glucose.

When Brain is affected, it causes

* Weakness of legs
* Double/blurred vision
* Confusion
* Headache
* Drowsiness

Adrenalin hormone—causes

* Sweating
* Rapid heart beat
* Feeling of panic and anxiety

Most people find it hard to describe how they feel but the proof is that the blood glucose is low.

What can cause hypoglycaemia

Common cause

* People who take medicines for control of Diabetes
* People who take anti-malarials or pain killers frequently
* Alcohol can cause hypoglycaemia specially in the early morning if food was not taken along with drinks in the night.

How to Prevent

Most important aspect is correction of diet. Modification of eating habits may help in resolving this problem. Change in lifestyle and behavioural modification may also help in correcting it.

One should avoid concentrated sugars/carbohydrates because 2 hours after consuming these preparations there is again rebound hypoglycaemia. By using concentrated carbohydrate preparations there is over-production of insulin which further reduces blood sugar levels.

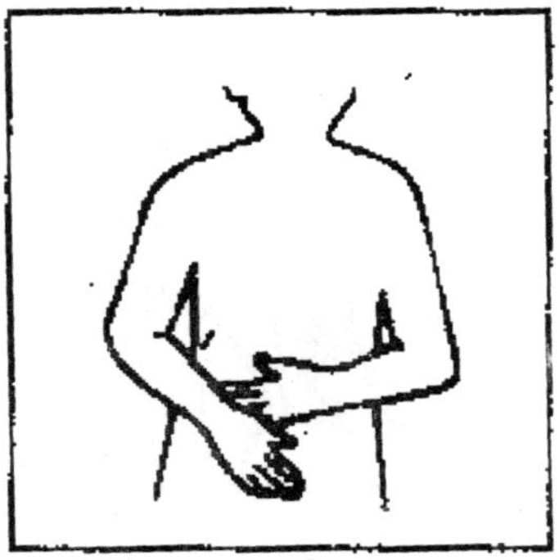

Hunger Pains

Trembling and Sweating

Blurred Vision

Headache

Giddiness

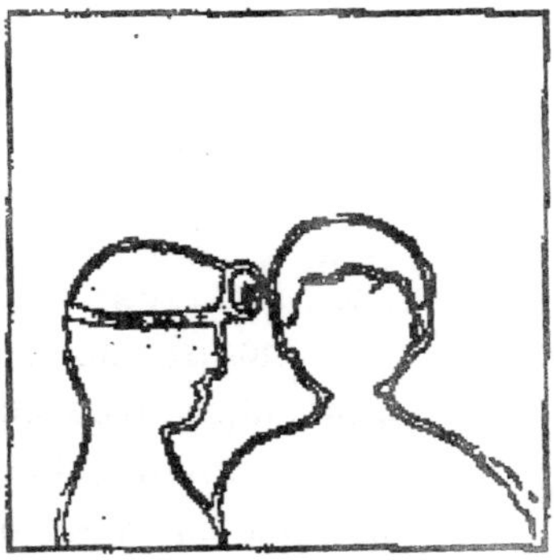

If you have all these Symptoms
Contact Doctor

Eat something before Exercise

Keep Family Members informed about Symptoms of Hypoglycaemia

What to do

1. Avoid refined sugars i.e. Sugar, Jaggery, Honey, Jam, chocolates, Sweet Potatoes and Biscuits.
2. Can use complex carbohydrates which include fruits (papaya), cereals and vegetables like pumpkin etc.
3. Food with high fibre content can be used. Beans and peas may be consumed frequently.
4. Frequent small meals may help in keeping blood sugar levels in normal range.
5. Alcohol should be avoided. If one can't resist this, he should not take more than one or two drinks (30 ml each) and that too over a period of 3 to 4 hours time along with snacks followed by meals/dessert.
6. Smoking during these episodes should be avoided as it may increase the problem by increasing heart rate, sweating and trembling.
7. Avoid sweets, ice cream and chocolates as they will increase weight.
8. Most persons take sugar, glucose, sweets to get rid of this problem but it rebounces/relapses because there is more insulin release which produces hypoglycaemia. So one should avoid sugar mixers. Persons having symptoms of low blood sugar should avoid religious fasting.

Diabetic Coma
(Hyperglycaemia)

Diabetic Coma, Ketoacidosis

When Blood Sugar levels are high patient becomes dull, feels extremely weak, vomiting, feels sleepy, skin is dry and breathlessness and Drowsiness followed by coma (unconciousness).

Warning signs

- — If one gets more and more desire for food and increased thirst.
- — Increased frequency of micturition.
- — Sudden Loss of Weight.
- — Feeling more sleepy and drowsy than usual.
- — Vomiting and pain in Abdomen.
- — Smell of over-ripe fruits in breath.
- — Fast and deep breathing.
- — Urine examination will reveal ketones.

Why this Happens (Seen under following circumstances)

1. If diabetic patients eat more and more and irregular in taking medicines.
2. Usually seen in Type I Diabetes, in children who may forget to take Insulin or during some infections when Blood Sugar levels rise very rapidly.
3. It can be seen in Adults too during stressful situations, infections or in persons who are alcoholic and absolutely irregular in taking medicines and food.

Symptoms

1. Weakness.
2. Excessive thirst.
3. Increased Appetite.
4. Increased Urination.
5. Dry skin.
6. Breathlessness.
7. Pain in Abdomen and distension.
8. Vomiting.
9. Nausea.
10. Drowsiness.
11. Disorientation and unconsciousness followed by coma. Blood-Sugar Test will reveal very high Blood sugar.

Urine will show—ketones (Normal urine will not show ketones)

Prevention and Treatment

All diabetic patients should know about hyperglycaemia and diabetic coma. Parents and relatives should be told about warning signs of diabetic coma. So that appropriate steps could be taken to prevent it. Patients should be shifted to hospital immediately where proper treatment can be given.

Insulin therapy along with other measures can save the life. So delay in shifting patient to good Medical Centre/Hospital should be avoided.

Hyperglycaemia (High Blood Sugar)

Causes

1. Not enough medication.
2. Too much carbohydrate in food.
3. Increase in weight.
4. Lack of activity.
5. Illness.
6. Stress.

Management

1. Check medications or seek medical advice.
2. Review diet.
3. Review diet and activity level.
4. Seek medical advice.
5. Review causes of stress.

- ❒ Diabectic ketoacidosis is an emergency.
- ❒ Do not take it lightly. Contact your doctor immediately.

  Symptoms are:
  - Excessive, urination and thirst
  - Nausea, vomiting and abdominal pain
  - Deep, rapid breathing with a fruity smell
  - Mental confusion.
- ❒ Blood/urine testing will reveal high sugar levels and presence of ketones.

Diabetes Ketoacidosis in Children

* If your diabetes is untreated or poorly controlled, blood glucose levels rise very high (hyperglycaemia).
* This occurs because you don't have enough insulin, the glucose in the blood is not being taken into the cells, so your body makes its own fuel by burning up stored fat.
* When fat is used in this way, waste products called ketones are produced and these excreted in the urine.
* Small amounts of ketones are not harmful, and are normally produced when you start to burn up body fat...for example when you go on a weight reduction diet.

However, problem arises when Blood Sugar levels are high and excessive ketones are produced and these start to accumulate in the body.

If untreated this will result in a condition called 'ketoacidosis'.

This condition is serious and urgent medical treatment is essential.

What causes this?

1. Illness and infection (e.g. flu, vomiting, diarrhoea, urine infections).
2. Missed or incorrect insulin dosage.
3. Poor injection technique.
4. Ineffective insulin due to faulty storage or expired date.

Watch for

1. The common signs and symptoms of hyperglycaemia, e.g. excessive urination and thirst, dry mouth and skin, tiredness.

2. Persistant high level of sugar in blood or urine.
3. Presence of ketones in the urine.
4. Nausea, vomiting and abdominal pain.
5. Sweet smell of acetone in the breath.
6. Respiration is deep and rapid.
7. Altered levels of consciousness.

To Prevent Ketoacidosis

If you are sick

1. Take your usual dose of insulin.
2. Test your Blood Sugar level and urine ketones at least 4 hourly (or more often if necessary).
3. Contact your Doctoı with your results.
4. Give extra quick acting insulin according to your doctor's guidelines.

If you cannot contact your Doctor, follow these guidelines:

(a) If your Blood Sugar Level (BSL) is less than 260 mg/100ml, continue your normal insulin.
(b) If your Blood Sugar Level (BSL) is between 260 mg% to 360 mg% give 4 units of quick acting insulin (Hum insulin-r or Actrapid) every 4 hours, in addition to your usual dose.
(c) If your Blood Sugar Level (BSL) is above 360 mg/100 ml, give 4 units of quick acting insulin (Hum Insulin-r or Actrapid) every 2 hours, in addition to your usual dose.
(d) Follow this procedure until your BSL is less than 250mg/100ml of Blood.

5. If you don't feel like eating, replace your normal carbohydrate portions with simple carbohydrate fluids, fruit juice etc. if your Blood Sugar Level (BSL) is persistently above 250mg/100ml, sip unsweetened fluids only.

6. Take extra clear sugar-free fluids. You need to have 200-500ml/hour (depending on your body size and degree of dehydration).
7. If your BSL is persistently high or if you are vomiting, you must contact your Doctor or go to Hospital.

Do not Delay!

Children with diabetes are no more likely to develop sore throats or virus illnesses than any other child providing their diabetes is well controlled. When diabetes is first diagnosed, poorly controlled, diabetes during an infection, stress, or other illness, the body's need for insulin increases. This causes the Blood Sugar level to rise very high (hyperglycaemia). With this lack of insulin the body cells can no longer use the glucose as the main source of energy so the body makes its own fuel by burning up stored fats. When fat is used in this way, waste products called ketones are produced and these are excreted in the urine.

High Blood Sugar	+	Reduced Insulin	=	Stored Fat	→ Ketones
	Pancreas				→ Energy

However, a problem arises when Blood Sugar levels are high and excessive ketones are produced and these start to accumulate in the body. If untreated this will result in ketoacidosis.

Ketoacidosis

This condition is serious and urgent medical treatment is urgently needed.

Causes

1. Initial diagnosis.
2. Illness and infection (e.g. flu, vomiting, diarrhoea).
3. Missed or incorrect insulin dosage (including poor injection technique).
4. Long-term poor control and neglect.

Watch For

1. The common signs and symptoms of hyperglycaemia.
   — Excessive urination;
   — Thirst;
   — Tiredness;
   — Weight loss;
   — Signs of dehydration
     • dry mouth/skin;
     • sunken eyes.
2. Persistent high levels of Sugar in the blood or urine.
3. Presence of ketones in the urine.
4. Nausea, vomiting and abdominal pains, vomiting is always serious.
5. Sweet smell of acetone on the breath.
6. Respirations deep and rapid.
7. Altered level of consciousness.

These symptoms may develop over hours or days.

PREVENTING KETOACIDOSIS IN CHILDREN

To Prevent ketoacidosis

If you are sick

1. *Never Omit Insulin*—always take your usual dose.
2. *Test Blood Sugar and Urine Ketones*—Atleast every 2 hours and hourly is necessary.
3. *Contact Your Doctor*—give results of tests.
4. *Extra Insulin*—quick acting insulin may be needed according to your doctor's guidelines.

If you cannot contact your doctor follow these guidelines:

(a) If your Blood Sugar Level (BSL) is less than 200mg%, continue your normal insulin;

(b) If your BSL is between 280-360mg per 100 ml of Blood, give 2 units of quick acting insulin (Hum Insulin-r or Actrapid) every 4 hours, in addition to your usual dose;

(c) If your BSL is above 360mg/100ml of Blood, give 2 units of quick acting insulin every 2 hours in addition to your usual dose;

(d) Follow this procedure until your BSL is less than 280 mg%.

5. *Replace Normal Carbohydrate*—If you don't feel like eating, replace with simple carbohydrate fluids, e.g. ordinary lemonade, fruit juice etc. If your BSL is persistently above 15mmol/L, sip carbohydrate free (unsweetened) fluids (lemon juice, mineral water).
6. *Extra Fluids*—You need to have extra carbohydrate free fluids every hour. (The amount depends on body size and degree of dehydration.)
7. *High BSL or Vomiting*—If BSL persistently high or you are vomiting you must contact your doctor or go to hospital.

Obesity or Over Weight

What is Obesity?

Obesity is the excessive accumulation of body fat i.e. more than 25 per cent of ideal body weight in boys and 32 per cent in girls. Worldwide, 51 per cent of women, 44 per cent of men and 30 per cent of children are overweight. At least one child in five is obese.

How do you come to know Whether you are Overweight, Obese or Normal Weight?

There is a scale called Body Mass Index (BMI) which is calculated from height and weight. This differs in male and female and for different age groups. The charts for the calculation can be availed.

Why do you become obese or overweight?

* Genetic — Family history of obesity or overweight
* Environmental
  - Sedentary lifestyle (No/minimal physical activity in daily life, watching TV, playing video games, working on computers, etc.)

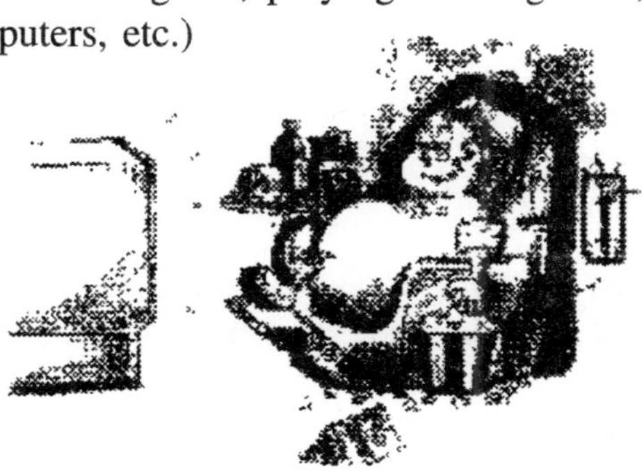

- Food Habits (Eating high fat, low fiber and high calorie diet like Burgers, Pizzas, French fries, Cola drinks etc.).

What can you do about it?

If you are not obese, not over weight.....Prevent both!

If you are over weight.......Reduce your weight and prevent obesity!

If you are obese.....Get rid of it!

How to get rid of Obesity?

Can be changed	*Can't be changed*
* Food Habits	* Genetic Background
* Physical activities	

Obesity Leads to—(1) Diabetes,
(2) Hypertension,
(3) Joint Problems.

Step by Step....

Food Habits — Eat the quantity (calories) only as much is needed for your daily activity. Neither less nor more.
Choose food high in fiber, low in fat which will help in controlling the quantity too.

Physical activity — Do physical activity which will consume calories on a regular basis. Use the leisure times for out door games instead of being Couch Potato.

Role of Teachers/School

- Planned, systematic inculcation of the above habits into children. Allocating certain fixed hours for guidance on nutrition in the curriculum.
- Discouraging the fast food outlets inside the school premises.

- Distribution of healthy dietary information for parents through children.
- Organizing dietary seminars for parents in the school.
- Encouraging healthy dietary stalls in school meals and annual functions.
- Encouraging children and giving awards to those children, who participate in Physical activity and Games.

Role of Parents

Children see their parents as their "Role Models" in life, hence it is of utmost importance to:

- Set examples by making healthy food choices and practicing physical activities at home on an ongoing basis.
- Explain the values of each food items and activities to children as much as possible.

Most Strange

It does seem strange however that there are campaigns against smoking, drinking and yet obesity which poses as a serious threat to life is brushed under the Carpet. It is not a "Sociable Topic".

That's why we thought of this project "Obesity Prevention At Grassroots Level."

"Never sit if you can stand
Never Stand if You can Walk
Never Walk if you can Run"

Diabetes and Heart Problems

One of the commonest causes of heart attack is diabetes mellitus and in majority of diabetes patients cause of death is heart attack. There are certain peculiarities of heart attack in these patients, as compare to heart attacks in non-diabetic patients.

— Incidence of heart attacks in diabetics is higher than general public.
— Incidence of heart attacks in diabetic males is 50 times higher while in females it is 10 times more.
— Incidence of sudden death due to Sudden Cardiac Arrest is 50 times more in males, while it is 300 times more in females in diabetics.
— 35 per cent of diabetic patients die due to heart problems before they reach the 55 years of age as compare to 4 to 8 per cent of general public.
— 50 per cent Diabetic patients have high blood pressure.

In obese diabetic patients blood cholesterol and triglyceride levels are high and these get deposited in the blood vessels which supply blood to heart. Because of this deposition blood supply to heart is affected (due to narrowing of blood vessels) and this can cause Angina or Heart Attack.

Other additional factors are:

— Obesity/Over weight.
— High Blood Pressure.
— Smoking.
— Blood vessels of legs, foot and arms also get narrowed down due to cholesterol deposition and can cause pain in legs while walking which may become better by

further walking. This is seen more frequently in Diabetics who are smoker.

Precautions

Certain precautions are essential—

- — Weight Records—reduce over weight.
- — Control Blood Pressure.
- — Swelling over legs and feet should be reported to Doctor.
- — Get regular sugar and cholesterol examinations and keep records.
- — Get X-Ray chest once in a year.
- — Get E.C.G. once in a year.
- — If one gets discomfort in chest while walking or after food, should undergo stress test/tread mill test so that cadiac status can be evaluated.

Bad Companions of Diabetes

- Hypertension (High Blood Pressure)
- Dyslipidaemia (High Cholesterol and Triglyceride Levels)
- Smoking
- Obesity/Over Weight/*Motapa*

All the above factors increase the risk for Strokes and Heart Attacks.

Hypertension (High Blood Pressure) is associated with:

- — Insulin Resistance,
- — Obesity Central, and
- — Accelerated Atherosclerosis (Blockage of arteries).

By keeping Blood Pressure under control, there was reduction in incidence of stroke by 44 per cent.

Blood Pressure should be kept around 130/82 to prevent vascular complication of Diabetes, mainly stroke and heart attacks.

As 40 per cent of diabetics have associated with high blood pressure, all diabetic patients should have regular blood pressure check up and if needed use medicines regularly as per their doctors advice.

Heart Attacks in Diabetics are seen in young diabetics and are usually severe. Heart attacks are painless (silent). Usually seen in the age group of 35 to 40 years. All the major blood vessels of Heart are involved. Always need By-Pass Surgery.

Instead of pain, they get discomfort in chest, suffocation and difficulty in breathing.

How to Cope

— Stop smoking.
— Keep Blood Sugar under control.
— Regular exercise and weight control.
— Control Blood Pressure.
— Regular Heart check up an follow your Doctor's advise.

By-Pass Surgery

— By-Pass Surgery would improve the quality of life make change in food habits and lifestyle.
— Persons can then lead a normal life.

Diabetes and Pregnancy

Diabetes does not spare anyone, let it be young or old, male or female, pregnant or non-pregnant female. Long back if a female was having many abortions, or was delivering abnormal or dead child it was presumed as God's *will*.

After many years of research and investigations the actual cause was identified. It is uncontrolled diabetes during pregnancy which is one of the causes of abortions.

Normally pregnant ladies have low levels of fasting blood sugar as compare to post prandial blood sugar which are little higher than normal.

Usually in pregnancy Insulin secretion is more but due to deficiency or defective production of Insulin, diabetes develops in pregnancy.

Growth of the organs of child usually takes place in 1st three months of pregnancy. During this period if Blood Sugar remains high, child will have congenital defects, like valvular heart defects absence of some parts of body or organs.

In other words pregnancy should be planned only once you are sure that there is no diabetes or if you have diabetes, it should be well controlled.

Uncontrolled diabetes in 2nd and 3rd trimester of pregnancy can cause mental retardation of child, size of head would be bigger and overall size of child may be big. Then mother can't deliver such a child normally and she has to under go Caesarean operation.

Therefore to avoid all this urine and blood tested for sugar.

Which group of ladies should undergo screening for Blood Sugar.

— All females with family history of diabetes.
— If urine sample shows sugar.
— H/o repeated abortions or still birth.
— H/o delivery of big size children.
— H/o delivery of child with congenital deformity.

Special blood test is available to detect the Blood Sugar Level pattern of last 2-3 months. This is done by estimation of Glycosylated haemoglobin. This test is specially helpful in planning motherhood and would indicate about the Blood Sugar Levels at the time of conception and before that.

Diagnosis

Screening and Diagnostic Criteria for Gestational Diabetes Mellitus

A. Screening for Gestational Diabetes

- 50 gm. oral glucose administered between 24th and 28th weeks, without regard to time of day or time of last meal.
- Venous plasma glucose measure one hour later.
- Value of 140 mg/100 ml or above in venous plasma indicates the need for a full diagnostic glucose tolerance test.

B. Diagnosis of Gestational Diabetes Mellitus

- 100 gm oral glucose load, administered in the morning after overnight fast lasting at least 8 hours but not more than 14 hours with normal diet and physical activity.
- Venous plasma glucose is measured fasting and at 1, 2 and 3 hours. Avoid exercise and smoking during this period.
- Two or more readings equal or more are diagnostic. Fasting 95 mg/100 ml, 1 hour—180 mg/100 ml, 2 hours—155 mg/100 ml, 3 hours—140 mg/100 ml.

Gestational Diabetes

What is gestational diabetes?

— Diabetes occurring for the first time in pregnancy.

— Onset is usually mid to late pregnancy.

— More common in those women:
  - whose relatives have diabetes
  - who are over 30 years
  - who are over weight

Why is it so important to maintain strict control of Blood Sugar?

— Poor diabetes control is associated with the risk of large babies with difficult labour.

— These babies may then have breathing problems and low Blood Sugar Levels at birth.

— Good diabetes control means a normal pregnancy and a normal delivery, with a healthy baby.

How will I know if my baby is doing well?

— Your Obstetrician will closely monitor your baby's progress. The baby's growth and development will be checked by Ultrasound examination.

— With good diabetes control you can expect a *normal* labour and delivery. Sometimes, it is necessary to induce labour a little earlier. If the baby is too big, a Caesarian Section may be necessary.

— After the birth, your baby will be watched closely in the Special Care Nursery for 24 to 48 hours to ensure the Blood Sugar Levels stay normal.

Should I take any special precautions after my pregnancy?

— You should have a Glucose Tolerance Test after the birth of your baby, to ensure a return to normal.

— Have a Blood Sugar Level done at least once a year.

— Be aware that you have a greater risk of developing Gestational Diabetes in future pregnancies.

— You have a greater risk developing Diabetes later in life (usually non-insulin dependent diabetes).

Is there anything I can do to prevent diabetes in later life?

— Continue with your diet (after adjustment by a Dietitian).
— Maintain ideal body weight for your height.
— Exercise to stay fit.

How to Manage

One should plan delivery only in hospital in such cases so that life of both mother and child can be safe.

Ultrasound examination will help to find out if there is any congenital defect so that appropriate precaution may be taken.

In Type II diabetes pregnant lady is aware about her being diabetic still she is reluctant to stop tablets. Pregnant ladies should not take any tablets for diabetes because these tablets are harmful to the foetus. Only safe and best treatment available is regular injection of Insulin. Pregnant diabetic lady requires one or two injections of plane Insulin. Newer available humane insulins are safe. Patient may require one or two injections depending upon Blood Sugar Levels.

Other factors are also essential in the treatment apart from insulin injections.

About Diet

In a pregnant lady there is on increase in weight per week, in the range of 300-400gm.

- Food should provide proper nutrition to both mother and child for growth.
- Should not increase extra weight.
- Should keep Blood Sugar Levels under control.
- Should provide 30-40 calories per kg. of normal weight.

Exercise—Should go for regular walk.

Diabetes and Eyes
Eye Disease Diabeties Complications

The Eye

The eye is a complex organ that makes sight possible. Light enters the eye through the pupil and passes through the lens. This focuses the light before it travels through a gel-like material called the vitreous. At the back of the eye, the light hits the retina and is changed to an image. This image travels to the brain through the optic nerve. Just off the center of the retina is the macula, the area of sharpest vision.

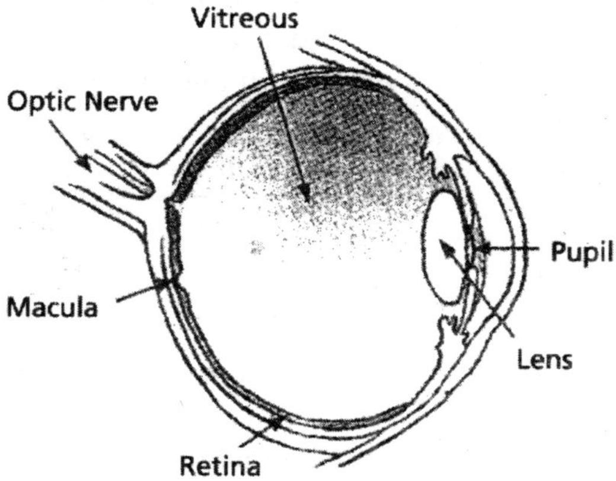

Eye Disease

The most common diabetes complication of the eye is retinopathy. This is damage to the small blood vessels of the retina. High blood glucose causes this damage over time. High blood pressure places extra force on the vessels, causing further damage. Abnormal cholesterol is also a factor that affects blood flow in the eye.

Cataracts and glaucoma are eye problems that are more common in people with diabetes. A cataract is the clouding of the lens; this clouding blocks the entry of light to the eye. Glaucoma is an increase in eye pressure that can damage the retina and optic nerve.

Retinopathy

Retinopathy can range from mild to severe. Its severity depends on the amount and type of damage to the blood vessels of the eye. The physical and visual changes that can happen are shown in the table below.

Mild/Nonproliferative Retinopathy (most common)

Physical Changes	*Visual Changes*
• Blood vessels become leaky	• Usually no change
• Swelling occurs	• Vision may become blurred if swelling (edema) affect the macula
• Less oxygen gets to the retina (This can lead to growth of abnormal vessels to compensate).	

Severe/proliferative Retinopathy (less common)

Physical Changes	*Visual Changes*
• Abnormal growth of new blood vessels that are weak and bleed easily	• There may be lasting vision loss, including blindness
• Heavier bleeding may occur in the vitreous	
• Scar tissue may form	
• Scar tissue can shift and pull the retina off the back of the eye.	

Symptoms of Retinopathy

Even with severe retinopathy, you may have no symptoms. However, if you notice any of the changes below, do not ignore them.

Sudden Changes

- Dark, floating spots (especially many new ones)
- "Cobwebs" that block vision
- Vision loss, especially in one eye (Check your vision one eye at a time.)

Gradual Changes

- Blurred vision
- Straight lines that appear bent
- Trouble reading, watching TV, driving
- Vision changes that come and go

Although floaters and blurring are common symptoms of retinopathy, they may not signal eye disease. Changes in blood glucose levels can cause blurring. Floating spots are more common as people age. It is best to see your doctor to be sure.

Your Health provider's Role

If your blood pressure is high, your provider may prescribe medications to help keep it in target. This helps to protect not only the eyes, but also the heart, blood vessels, and kidneys. Medications to keep cholesterol in check can also limit damage to eye vessels.

Your provider can refer you to an ophthalmologist (eye specialist) to screen you for eye disease on a yearly basis. During the exam, the provider will dilate (widen) your pupils to check your retinas and inner eyes for problems. The provider will also check for cataracts and perform a simple test for glaucoma.

You may need to see a retina-specialist about diabetes related eye disease. To check for blood vessel problems in the back of the eye, this specialist may order an eye photograph. To do this, dye is injected into your arm and travels through your blood vessels to your eyes. This helps eye vessels show up in the photograph.

Ongoing Treatment

Eye problems can be treated as follows.

Laser therapy. Lasers (beams of light flashed at the retina) can seal leaking blood vessels or control the growth of abnormal vessels. Often, a series of laser treatments over time is needed. Laser treatment can stop eye disease from getting worse. However, it cannot usually bring back lost vision. (Vision may improve somewhat if excess blood clears from the eye).

Vitrectomy. If there is a lot of bleeding and scarring in the eye , an operation called a vitrectomy can help. The surgeon removes bloody inner eye fluid (vitreous) and any scars that have formed. Done early, vitrectomy has a high success rate. Surgery to repair a detached retina is also possible, but is not as successful.

Cataract surgery. An eye surgeon can remove the cloudy lens and replace it with a new, clear lens.

Glaucoma treatment. Eye drops, pills, laser treatment, or surgery can help drain excess fluid from the eye to relieve pressure.

Low-vision aids and adaptive tools. If you have partial vision loss that can't be restored magnifiers and other items can help you. There are also special tools for managing your diabetes, such as blood glucose meters with large print displays.

One of the most important and sensitive organ of the body is Eyes. In diabetes, eyes, like any other organ of body, are involved and can cause complete blindness.

Involvement of eyes depend upon the duration of diabetes. If diabetes is there for more than 15 years eyes are definitely involved.

Eyes are more involved in Type I diabetes than Type II diabetes. Other factor which is responsible for eye involvement is uncontrolled Blood Sugar. Prolonged period of uncontrolled diabetes causes more danger to eyes.

Symptoms are

— Irritation and Itching in eyes.

— Watering and painful eye movements.

— Headache, redness, diminished vision.
— Double vision, black spots in front of eyes.
— Frequent change in power of glasses.
— Paralysis of eye muscles leading to double vision or squint.
— Cataract, and sudden loss of vision—due to bleeding in eye or retinal detachment.

How to Manage

Best and simple way to keep the diabetes under control is by strict diet control and regular use of anti-diabetic medicines.

— All diabetic patients should have regular complete eye check up at least once in a year.
— Diabetics who smoke are at a higher risk for loss of eye sight.
— Blood pressure should be kept under control.
— Retinal detachment and retinopathy can be kept under control by photo coagulation and laser therapy which is very effective. This type of treatment is available at all big centres. It is prophylactic therapy and can prevent blindness in Diabetic patients.

Eye Care in Diabetes

When you have diabetes, you have a high risk of eye problems that can lead to severe damage or blindness. This risk becomes even higher if you are between 40 to 60 years old age if you have had diabetes for a number of years.

What is especially bad is that many times the eyes are damaged before any symptoms are felt. So it is very important to visit your eye doctor regularly (at least once a year)—and immediately if you notice anything wrong with your eyes.

Common Eye Problems in Diabetics

1. *Cataracts*—Clouding of the normally clear lens in the eye.

2. *Glaucoma*—An increase in pressure within the eye.
3. *Diabetic retinopathy*—Weakening and breaking down of the small blood vessels in the retain.

Eye Care Do's	*Eye Care Don'ts*
• Wear goggles or safety glasses if eyes are at risk.	• Don't touch eyes with dirty fingers.
• Direct all spray nozzles away from eyes.	• Don't rub or overuse eyes.
• Read instructions on cosmetic liquids or Powders.	• Don't sit under sun-lamp without goggles.
• Wear sun glasses on bright days (especially on sand, or snow).	• Don't use saliva to wet makeup or contact lenses.
• Get immediate treatment for red/painful eyes.	• Don't wear dirty contact lenses.
• Tell eye specialists you have diabetes.	• Don't try to remove particles from eyes; see an eye doctor.

Diabetes and Menopause

Are you a woman with diabetes who is approaching menopause? Is a member of your family, or someone close to you, at this stage? In either case, you may be concerned about how this transition affects women.

How Long Does The Menopause Usually Last?

Menopause, which signifies the end of menses, is a natural stage in a woman's life. Menopause is considered to have taken place after a lady has been "period free" for twelve months. Symptoms of menopause can start in early forties and continue for many years. Menopause itself usually occurs between age 48 and 55.

The symptoms of menopause include: Hot flushes, Night sweats, Changes in sex drive (either way), Dizziness, Fatigue, Sleep disturbances, irregular periods, mood swings, difficulty with memory, joint pains, palpitations of heart. About 15% of ladies get sufficient discomfort to require medical help.

Effects of Menopause On Diabetes

— Much higher risk of Heart Attacks and angina
— More frequent low blood sugar attacks, and
— Reduced insulin or medication requirement
— Weight gain
— Loss of bone mass (Bone Thinning)
— Rise of cholesterol
— Rise of Blood pressure

So just follow the basics of diabetes control with special emphasis on weight control, Fat intake control and re adjustment of antidiabetic medication with your diabetologist's advice.

Dental Care in Diabetes

Oral Health Problems

Diabetes Complications

Healthy teeth and gums are part of a healthy digestive system. Oral health problems can affect your nutrition and your enjoyment of food. High blood glucose causes the natural bacteria in your mouth to multiply. This puts you at greater risk for gum disease and other oral health problems. Not only can high blood glucose lead to gum disease, but gum disease can also raise blood glucose levels.

Gum Disease

We all have natural bacteria in our mouths. These bacteria, along with food and saliva, create a sticky film called plaque. When plaque is not cleaned daily from our teeth and gums, it can harden and become tartar. A dental cleaning can remove tartar. If left on the teeth, tartar can get under the gums to damage teeth and the bone underneath. This is gum disease, the most common oral health complication of diabetes.

Progression of Gum Disease

Plaque and tartar

Oral bacteria multiply to form plaque on teeth, if not removed, plaque hardens into tartar.

Gingivities (early gum disease)

Plague and tartar stick to teeth and start to push gums away. Gums swell and bleed.

Periodontitis (advanced gum disease)

Tartar is under the gum line. Gums pull away from the teeth and their roots. Tooth and bone damage follows. Teeth may fall out or need to be removed.

Symptoms of Gum Disease

Watch for these symptoms, even though they may not be obvious in early gum disease.

- Gums that are red, tender, and swollen
- Visible tartar on your teeth
- Gums that bleed easily
- Pus at the gum line
- Gums that pull away from the teeth
- A bad taste in your mouth
- Persistent bad breath
- A change in your bite or in the fitting of partial dentrues

Other Oral Complications

Dry Mouth. This is a lack of saliva, which keeps the mouth wet and helps in cleaning. The cause may be high blood glucose, autonomic nerve damage, or medications. Dry mouth can lead to cavities, irritation, and infection in mouth.

Thrush (fungal infection). This fungus is common in your body and is usually under control. However, high blood glucose can feed the fungus. Antibiotics can also help thrush to thrive. It can worsen, too, with smoking and wearing a denture.

Damage to the sense of taste. This may be caused by poor oral care, gum disease, and oral infections.

Bacteria from gum disease in the blood-stream. Bacteria from gum disease can travel to other parts of your body. If you have damaged heart valves, bacteria can stick to them. Bacteria can also settle in other organs. This can lead to severe infections. Bacteria in the bloodstream can also make it harder to control blood glucose levels.

Symptoms of Oral Health Problems

- Dark spots on the teeth
- White or red patches on soft tissues
- Sores or infections
- Mouth or sinus pain
- Tooth sensitivity
- A burning sensation on the tongue
- Difficulty in swallowing
- Fever or high blood glucose with no apparent cause

Your Provider's Role

Your primary care provider can check your mouth for general problems and refer you to a dentist.

During your regular dental exam, your dentist and hygienist should:

- Check your mouth for signs of irritation or other problems
- Show you proper brushing and flossing methods
- Find and remove plaque and tartar
- Clean and polish your teeth

Possible tests may include:

- X-rays
- Other diagnostic tests, such as periodontal charting (measuring the pockets between teeth and gums)

Your primary provider and your dentist should work as a team. For example, dental work may require an antibiotic or other medication. Both providers should consider how the new drugs might interact with other medications you are taking.

On-going Treatment

If you have gum disease, your dentist may scrape the roots of your teeth to remove hidden tartar. This requires local anesthesia.

If damage is more advanced, you may be referred to a periodontist (gum specialist) for surgery to rebuild bone and gum tissue. Tooth removal may even be required. If so, you may need a bridge or dentures.

You may need medication to treat dry mouth, infections, and sores. Using sugarless gum, mints, water, or ice chips can help dry mouth. Restricting caffeine and alcohol is also helpful. Saliva substitutes are another option.

Damage to the sense of taste may improve with better glucose control and changes to your food plan. Better oral care can help control your blood glucose. Check with your diabetes care team for help with ways to improve taste sensation.

* Brush and floss after every meal and before bed time.
* Use of soft-bristled brush and unwaxed floss.
* Brush all surfaces of all teeth.
* Lightly brush your tongue.
* Massage your gums gently with finger or brush.
* Use fluoride tooth-paste.
* Eat a well-balanced diet.
* Avoid foods high in sugar, especially foods that stick to teeth like raisins, caramel, and other chewy candies.
* Visit your Dentist every three months for cleaning, polishing, inspection, and oral hygiene instruction.

Nerve Involvement in Diabetes

Diabetes involves all the nerves and muscles of body. Numbness in feet, tingling, burning, sensations, pain in legs specially at night are all features of diabetic Neuropathy. Some patients will not be able to walk due to pain in legs or weakness once they sit down they can't get up without support.

Some people may feel difficulty in typing or writing and all movements of body become painful.

These are all signs of involvement of Nerves called as Neuropathy or Diabetic Neuritis. This damage is due to poor control and longer durations of diabetes. These symptoms are both Sensory (Burning, tingling, numbness) and Motor (weakness and wasting of muscles).

All these symptoms, i.e. Sensory and Motor are the result of uncontrolled Diabetes and patient usually responds well once Blood Sugar is controlled either by medicines or by Insulin injections.

Some persons may have diminished sweating in the feet or increased sweating over upper part of body.

Some persons will have constipation. Others will have intermittent watery diarrhoea especially at night or other will have distension of abdomen.

Some Diabetic patients have Urinary and sexual problems also like:

— Difficulty in passing urine.
— Repeated urine infections.
— Difficulty in holding urine.

Impotence, i.e. unability to achieve or sustain erection satisfactorily for sexual intercourse. This is one of the commonest problem faced by diabetic patients. Yet for months and years they won't discuss it with their doctor. Most of the time either doctor is too busy or patient is with family members so he is not able to express the problem to doctor. Longer the duration of uncontrolled Diabetes, more and more would be Sexual problems. Some patients may request their doctor for some magic pill or injection. Some people may try Alcohol or other drugs—but all these may aggravate the agony of patient.

Treatment

1. Psychological counselling to both partners.
2. Stop use of Alcohol.
3. Strict Diabetes control.
4. There are certain devices—suction technique erection can be maintained—(suction pumps are available).
5. Injections of Papaverine before intercourse can cause sustained erection. However, these all techniques have side effects of infections etc., and should be under strict medical supervision.

For all Neurological problems arising due to uncontrolled diabetes the best treatment is to keep Blood Sugar under control and consult your doctor before trying for any magic pill.

Skin and Sexual Problems in Diabetes

Skin Problems

About 30 to 35 per cent of Diabetic patients develop skin problems. Because of Diabetes the severity of these infections is more as compare to the non-diabetic.

Diabetic patients develop finger infections of nails, nail bed, between fingers, inner and part of thigh or at private parts. Sometimes itching and rash may be presenting symptom of Diabetes in females specially if she is over weight. In males, cuts at glans penis indicate increase in Blood Sugar.

Sometimes Diabetic patient will have oral ulcers or thrush. Fingers infection of nails may cause swelling and performation at one side of nail or destruction of nail. Sometimes there are ulcers between fingers or toes and it may be so much painful that one cannot wear shoes.

Diabetic men present with redness and swelling of the glans penis and it is usually associated with sever itching and pain. This is called as Balanitis. There may be difficulty in retracting skin.

In some Diabetic patients because of these problems, circumcision is advised.

In all above skin problems antifungal lotions and creams help in solving the problem. All above conditions indicate that the Blood Sugar is not under control and it has to be kept in control.

Sexual Problems in Diabetes

Diabetes is one of the few diseases that can cause impotence, i.e. loss of the ability to achieve and maintain an erection hard enough for sexual intercourse—also called as Erectile Dysfunction (ED).

Erectile Dysfunction is 3 times more common among diabetics than in the healthy control population. Incidence varies from 28 to 59 per cent.

Sexual Dysfunction

When a man gets sexually excited, his brain and nerves signal his penis to fill with blood. This makes his penis erect. When a woman gets sexually excited, her brain and nerves signal her vagina to swell with blood and become lubricated. These changes prepare men and women for sexual intercourse.

Damage to the blood vessels can reduce blood flow (circulation) to the genitals. Damage to the nerves can reduce sensation or feeling in the genitals. Both of these conditions can limit the body's sexual response. They can also make it difficult to reach orgasm. These changes can affect both women and men.

Emotions can also play a role in sexual function. For example, worrying about sexual complications can affect sexual function. Worrying that blood glucose may go too low during sex can limit desire. Physical problems can lead to less interest in sex. They can also cause anxiety about performance.

The physical and emotional problems described above can affect both sexes. The next panel details the physical problems unique to each sex.

Conditions and Symptoms

Men and women experience sexual dysfunction differently. The major conditions and symptoms are explained below.

Erectile dysfunction (impotence)

At first, the penis may be less firm during arousal. Later, it can be more difficult for the penis to maintain firmness during sex. Eventually, having an erection may be impossible.

Retrograde ejaculation

During an orgasm, little or no semen is released from the penis. Instead, semen is released into the bladder.

Vaginal dryness

Lack of vaginal lubrication can cause irritation or pain during intercourse.

Yeast (fungal) infection and vaginitis inflammation)

Itching, burning, and unusual vaginal discharge are the primary symptoms of these conditions. They can cause discomfort during intercourse. They can also affect desire.

Bladder problem

Infection, pain, or fear of urine leakage can affect sexual pleasure.

Your Provider's Role

Sexuality is an important part of life. Yet, for many people it can be hard to talk about. Sharing your concerns about your sexual health is the best way to help your provider dignose and treat your condition. Your provider will probably check:

- To make sure your blood glucose, blood pressure, and cholesterol are in target
- For nerve damage and circulatory problems
- For vaginal and urinary tract infections (women)
- To see if your medications may be causing side effects
- For hormone deficiency
- For physical problems not related to diabetes (such as injury or complications of surgery)
- If tobacco and alcohol use may be causing your problems

Your provider may also refer you to a sexual health specialist, sexual therapist, gynecologist (for women), or urologist (for men). These providers may perform other tests or provide counseling to address any emotional concerns about sexual dysfunction.

Ongoing Treatment

Your provider will continue to monitor your blood glucose levels, blood pressure, and cholesterol. There are also treatments that can help. These are listed in the table on the next panel.

Men

Condition	*Treatment*
Erectile dysfunction	• Pills (Viagra*, Levitra*, Cialis*) • Injections to increase blood flow • Penile (uretral) suppositories • Penile rings • Vacuum pumps • Penile (surgical) implants
Retrograde ejaculation	• No true treatments, but a specialist can assist if fertility is an issue

Women

Condition	*Treatment*
Vaginal dryness	• Lubricants • Hormone supplementation
Yeast infections	• Antifungal medications
Vaginitis	• Topical treatments, medications
Bladder problems	• Antibiotics (for infections) • Urination before and after intercourse

Men and Women

Condition	*Treatment*
Medication side effects	• Different medications that don't affect sexual function (if possible)
Hormone deficiency	• Hormone supplementation
Psychological needs	• Counseling
Reduced sensation	• Work with your partner; communicate; experiment

Predictive Factors

Age, duration of diabetes, levels of Blood Sugar, presence of complications especially Retinopathy and Neuropathy, high blood pressure and drugs taken for controlling it, smoking and alcohol abuse. Risk of impotence is high in diabetics where Blood Sugar are on very high side and HbA1c is more than 9.8%. Persistent

high blood glucose leads to certain chemical changes which damage arteries and nerves.

Initially, there is diminished Penile rigidity and reduced ability to sustain an erection. This progress to full-fledged failure of Erection. Very often, sexual desire persists.

Psychological factors

There is substantial evidence to suggest that Erectile Dysfunction in diabetes is often Psychological in origin. Factors are: awareness of suffering from a chronic condition, relationship problems and fear of failure during sexual intercourse. Many patients don't discuss this problem with their doctor. Only 50% of diabetics having sexual problems discuss with their doctor about it.

How to Manage

First and the most important aspect of treatment is to control Blood Sugar by diet or drug treatment and by persuading the patient to abstain from risk factors like smoking and alcohol abuse.

Psychotherapy care help to minimize the anxiety and modify the couple's sexual habits in helpful way.

FREQUENTLY ASKED QUESTIONS FOR ERECTILE DYSFUNCTION (ED)

Sexual Problems in Diabetes by Men

Q. 1. What is an Erectile Dysfunction?

Ans. Erectile Dysfunction is the persistent inability for a man to achieve and maintain an erection for a complete and satisfactory sexual activity. Previously it was also called as impotence, which had negative connotation. But, now the term used is Erectile Dysfunction which describes the medical problem more accurately and with a precise clinical description.

Q. 2. How Common is ED among Men?

Ans. Do not panic if you have erectile dysfunction, as you are not the only one suffering. It is a fairly common condition encountered by many. But for a large number of men ED is a frequent problem. An estimated 100 million are affected by this dysfunction.

Q. 3. Does ED Affect the sexual desires?

Ans. No, normally it does not affect the arousal, desire and ejaculation. Erectile Dysfunction means only an inability to obtain or maintain an erection, but has no effect on desire.

Q. 4. Can Erectile Dysfunction be assessed and treated?

Ans. Yes, ED is easily assessed and treated. A detailed history taken from the patient is the most important aspect of diagnosing the ED. For most patients investigation/assessment is limited to bare minimum that is blood pressure and examination of external genitalia. Doctor, will advice you if further tests and investigations are required.

Q.5. What are the treatment options available?

Ans. The treatment option available are intracavernosal prostaglandin injection, transurethral alpostadil (suppository), vacuum devices and oral sildenafil therapy. Your physician will advice you on the treatment schedule.

Q.6. Is oral drug therapy effective?

Ans. Oral drug therapy with sildenafil has shown to be effective in treating men with ED. Improvement is erectile response has been observed 50 to 80 per cent of patient.

Q.7. What is sildenafil used for?

Ans. Sildenafil is only used for treatment in men who have difficulty in having and/or maintaining an erection for a complete sexual intercourse, in other words, it is used to treat impotence or erectile dysfunction in men.

Q.8. How does sildenafil action occur in the body?

Ans. An erection is a result of a delicate but perfectly balanced process that involves the brain, blood vessels, nerves and hormones. The penis is specifically designed to respond to the change that occur when a person is sexually aroused. In the penis an erection occurs as a result of an increase in blood flow into the internal area. Sildenafil increases men's ability to achieve and maintain erection during sexual arousal.

Q.9. How to use the medicine?

Ans. The drug sildenafil should be taken an hour before you have sex. It may take longer for the medicine to work if it is taken with a high fat meal. The medicine should be stored at room temperature away from direct light, heat and moisture. This medicine should be kept away from children.

Q.10. When the medicine should not be used?

Ans. If you are allergic to sildenafil, than you should not use the drug. It should not be used if you are taking nitrate containing medication that is isosorbide, dinitrate, glyceryl trinitarate etc.

Q. 11. What if I am on some other medication?

Ans. If you are taking some medicine for other ailments, it is best to discuss the problem with your doctor. He will be able to advise you.

Q.12. Does sildenafil have any side effects?

Ans. As with most of the drugs some people have side effects others have none. The most common side effect reported by men who have used the drug were: headache, flushing, stomach ache and mild and temporary visual changes. If an erection that lasts longer than four hour, which is rare, consult your doctor.

Q.13. How many times is the drug taken?

Ans. Sildenafil is used when you want to have an erection. It should be used only one time each day and not more often.

Q. 14. Can everyone take Sildenafil?

Ans. Sildenafil is for men who have erectile dysfunction. It will not make a normal erection last longer or occur more often. Therefore, this medicine is not recommended for men who have normal sexual functions.

Q. 15. What about new Drug?

Ans. New drug Tadalafil is now available for use. 10 mg of this salt is taken prior to anticipated sexual activity and without regard to food. Efficacy of Tadalafil persists upto 24 hours post dose.

People with Angina, Heart Attacks, Low Blood Pressure, Heart Failure and Stroke should not use this Drug.

Diabetes and Kidney Problems

Diabetes and Kidney

Diabetes is one of the most common disease which damages kidney. Every year large number of diabetic patients undergo dialysis and renal transplants. In Type I diabetes 30 per cent patients suffer from Kidney damage if diabetes was detected before the age of 15 years. In NIDDM or Adult type of Diabetes incidence is lower it is about 15 to 20 per cent.

Kidney Disease

The body has two kidneys. They filter extra fluid and waste products from the blood. The bladder holds the liquid waste created by the kidneys until it leaves the body during urination.

Kidney disease, or nephropathy, is a loss of kidney function over time. High blood glucose levels cause damage to the tiny blood vessels in the kidneys. This reduces their ability to remove waste. High blood pressure also damages these vessels and can cause or worsen kidney disease. At the same time, kidney disease can worsen high blood pressure.

Kidney disease can be prevented and treated by keeping blood glucose levels and blood pressure in target. Unchecked, kidney disease will progress. In the most serious cases, the kidneys stop working.

Symptoms

Kidney disease develops slowly. At first, there are no symptoms, but your provider can check for signs such as protein in your urine and high blood pressure. If early kidney disease is not detected and treated, the following may develop—

- Swelling (edema)
  —Starting in the feet and lower legs
  —Slowly moving to the upper legs and waist
  —In more advanced cases, moving to the hands, face, and eyes.
- Tiredness or weakness due to anemia (low red blood cell count)
- More frequent urination overnight
- Poor appetite, nausea, vomiting
- Muscle cramps in the legs
- Itching

Many people think that back pain, urinary tract infections, or blood in the urine are symptoms of kidney disease. You will want to mention these to your provider, but they are often not signs of kidney changes related to diabetes.

Progression of Kidney Disease

Even if you have no symptoms, this is how kidney disease progresses.

Early Kidney Disease	*Treatment*
• Protein in the urine (microalbuninuria) • Increased risk for heart and blood vessel disease	• Blood glucose and blood pressure control are critical • An ACE inhibitor or an ARB (blood pressure medication) helps protect the kidneys even if blood pressure is normal
Later Kidney Disease	*Treatment*
• Decreased function of the kidneys • Increased protein in the urine (macroalbuminuria) • Increased blood pressure • Increased creatinine and urea (waste products) in the blood	• Blood glucose control • Additional blood pressure medications as needed • Medication for abnormal cholesterol as needed • Dietary changes as advised by dietician.
End-Stage Kidney Disease	*Treatment*
• The kidneys stop working	• Dialysis • Kidney transplant

Your Provider's Role

Your provider needs to check your urine for protein (albumin) every year. This is usually measured along with urine creatinine (a waste product filtered by the kidneys). The test results are given as the amount of albumin per gram of alb/creatinine ratio.

Reading	*Urine Protein Level*	*Diagnosis*
Under 30 mg/g Cr	Normal	No kidney disease
30-300 mg/g Cr	Microalbuminuria (some protein)	Early kidney disease
Over 300 mg/g Cr	Macroalbuminuria Increased protein	Later kidney Disease

If you have two high readings (microalbuminuria) over a period of three to six months, you have early kidney disease. *Microalbuminuria also means that you have a greater risk of heart and blood vessels disease. Your provider should check all of your heart disease risk factors and treat those as needed.*

Other testes, such as a 24-hour urine test, may also be used to measure urine protein. Another kind of urine test (urinalysis) may be done to check for infections or other factors. That may affect your urine protein level.

If you have high blood pressure or early kidney disease, your provider will start you on an ACE inhibitor or an ARB. These medications lower blood pressure by keeping blood vessels open wider, particularly in the kidneys.

If you have type 1 diabetes, your first urine protein test is done about five years after diagnosis. If you have type 2 diabetes, you should be tested yearly from diagnosis on.

Ongoing Treatment

If you have advancing kidney disease, you may need a periodic blood test to determine your creatinine level. This is a measure of how well the kidneys are working. A normal serum (blood) creatinine level is usually less than 1.5 mg/100 mL. If your creatinine level is higher than normal or is moving up in the normal range, this may mean the kidneys aren't filtering waste products as well as they should.

Another measure of the kidneys' filtering function is the glomerular filtration rate (GFR). This may be used in addition to serum creatinine. It is often recommended for those with significant kidney changes. Normal GFR is greater than 90 mL/min. If the filtering ability of the kidneys is worsening, this number will drop over time. The GFR can be calculated using factors such as your weight, age, sex, and serum creatinine.

Even in later stages, there are ways to slow the progression of kidney disease. These include:

- Keeping your blood glucose and blood pressure in target range
- Taking a water pill (diuretic) and additional blood pressure pills
- Limiting foods that are high in salt, protein, phosphorus, or potassium (as needed)
- Treating abnormal cholesterol lavels with medication, such as a statin

If kidney disease continues to progress, the kidneys stop working. At this stage, the body needs help to remove waste. Dialysis, or filtering your blood with a machine, is one way to do this. A kidney transplant is the other option.

How to Prevent

1. Keep Blood Sugar under control.
2. If Blood Pressure is higher, the damage to kidney will be more so blood pressure should be controlled. Get regular check up and consult your doctor.
3. Proteins restriction is important. If urine start showing albumin reduce protein in take to 20 to 40 gm/day.
4. Don't take medicines without doctor's advice as all medicines have adverse effect on kidneys.
5. Get regular blood test for sugar, urea and creatinine because the results will indicate kidney status.
6. Stop smoking.

The Digestive System and Urinary Tract System

Your stomach mixes food with digestive juices and stomach acid. Food begins to break down and moves into the small intestine for further digestion. There nutrients from the food, including glucose, are absorbed into the bloodstream. Next, the large intestine absorbes water. The remaining material becomes waste (stool). This moves to the rectum. Sphincter muscles control when stool moves out of the rectum.

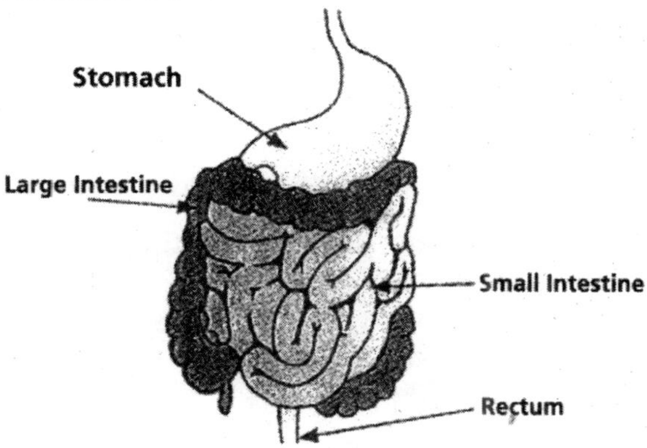

Nerve damage (autonomic neuropathy) can cause the digestive tract to slow down or speed up. This can lead to the following problems.

Gastroparesis

The food mixture stays in your stomach longer than normal before moving to the small intestine. As a result, it takes longer for glucose to enter your bloodstream. If you take your insulin or diabetes pill before eating, you will have insulin in your bloodstream, but not enough glucose. This can cause low blood glucose. When the glucose finally enters your bloodstream later, most of the insulin may be gone. This can cause high blood glucose.

Slow emptying of the stomach can also lead to nausea and vomiting.

Constipation. Waste material moves too slowly through your intestines. The result is less than three stools per week. This is the most common digestive complication.

Diarrhoea. Waste material moves too quickly through your intestines, especially after a large meal. As a result, less water is absorbed. This causes watery stools.

Stool Leakage. Nerve damage affects the sphincter muscles that control bowel movements.

Other digestive problems include trouble in swallowing, gallstones, and sweating on the upper chest and head while eating certain foods. This perspiration is called gustatory sweating.

The Urinary Tract

Your kidneys filter your blood to clear out natural waste. This liquid waste (urine) is stored in the bladder. When the bladder is full, your nerves let you know that it is time to urinate.

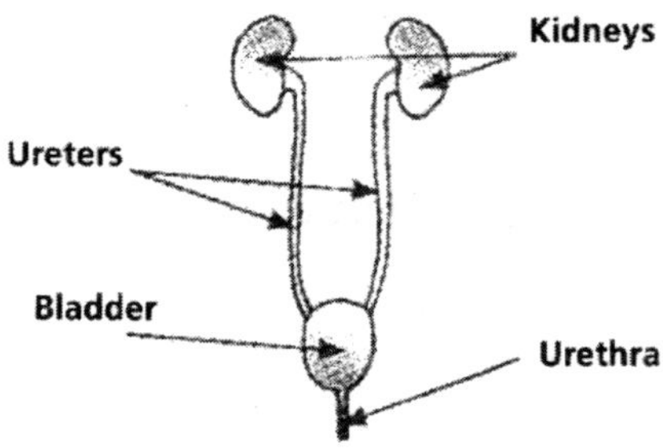

Nerve damage to your bladder can make it hard for you to sense when it is full or empty. Nerve damage can also affect the sphincter muscles that hold or release urine. If your bladder is full and you don't realize it, urine may leak out. On the other hand, you may not be able to tell if you've emptied your bladder completely. Urine that is left in the bladder can cause bladder enlargement, infection, and even kidney damage.

Symptoms

Nerve damage in these organs may create the following symptoms.

Stomach

Nause; vomiting of food eaten hours ego bloating, pain; heartburn; acid reflux; a feeling of fullness that comes on quickly, dehydration, unstable blood glucose levels; poor nutrition weight loss

Intestines

Unstable blood glucose levels, constipation, diarrhoea, stool leakage

Bladder

Urine leakage; difficult or slow urination; less frequent urination incomplete emptying, fullness in the lower abdomen

Bladder Infection

Cloudy; dark, strong smelling urine; blood in the urine, frequency urination in small amounts, burning or pain while urinating, the urge to urinate without success, tender lower back fever; chills; high blood glucose levels

Your Provider's Role

Your provider will do a physical exam and may order some diagnostic tests. This includes checking to see if your AIC is in target. Your provider will also review your medications. Some may have side effects that cause digestive or urnary problems. You may also get a referral to a gastroenterologist (stomach and intestine specialist) or a urologist (urinary tract specialist).

For Your Stomach or Intestines

Different tests can

- Check nerve and muscle activity of your stomach and intestines
- Determine how long food stays in your stomach
- Determine how quickly food moves through your intestines
- Check for excess bacteria in the small intestine or unhealthy bacteria in the large intestine
- Check for food allergies
- Check for intolerance to gluten—from wheat and other grains (This can happen in type 1 diabetes.)
- Rule out other disorders such as ulcers, tumors, or Crohn's disease

Your provider can prescribe medications to help reduce nausea and vomiting or to stimulate the stomach to empty. In addition, a dietitian may review and adjust your food plan to help reduce any problems you are having.

If medications fail to help, a gastric stimulator may be an option for those with gastroparesis. This small device is implanted like a pacemaker. The stimulation it produces can help reduce nausea and vomiting.

For Your Urinary Tract and Bladder

You may have tests to:

- Identify urinary tract infections
- Check kidney function
- View your bladder for structural problems
- Check your bladder for incomplete emptying

Medications can help bladder muscles relax. Others can help the bladder empty more completely. Antibiotics help treat urinary tract infections.

Your provider might also suggest that you do Kegel exercises on a regular basis. Strengthening pelvic floor muscles can help keep urine from leaking.

Emergency in Diabetes

There are two types of situations when a Diabetic patient would need urgent medical care.

Hyperglycaemic coma	—	Very high Blood Sugar levels causing unconsciousness and coma.
Hypoglycaemia	—	Low Blood Sugar levels—causing unconsciousness and coma.

How a Common Man can Differentiate

Hyperglycaemic coma		*Hypoglycaemic coma*
Excessive thirst	—	Excessive Sweating Headache, Palpitation.
Urination, Dry skin Excessive Sugar in Urine	—	No sugar in Urine
Urine Test for Ketones is positive (+ve)	—	Test for ketones is negative (–ve).
Extreme weakness and pain in Abdomen	—	Trembling.
Rapid and deep breathing	—	No change.
Typical smell of over ripe fruits in breath	—	Nothing like this.
No response to sugar	—	Dissolve sugar and give orally patient becomes normal.
H/O missing injection and excess food intake.	—	H/O missing food but taken injection.

Diabetes in Old Age

NIDDM or Type II Diabetes is usually detected in majority of patients between 40 to 70 years of age. As such with advancing age there may be problems of joint pains, impaired vision, impaired hearing, mobility disorders, urinary problems due to enlarged prostate. For a long time he may attribute diabetic symptoms to aging process. It becomes obvious when for some surgery like cataract, or for dental problem he undergoes investigation and then it is revealed that he is suffering from Diabetes. On further questioning he may complain of frequency of urination. He may give a vague history of some family member suffering from Diabetes. As such there are other problems of joint pains, backache, defective vision and uncontrolled diabetes, in the presence of these problems, become worse.

Due to Diabetes in elderly persons there could be

— Lack of Physical strength and impotency.
— Delayed healing of wound and repeated infections.
— High blood pressure, angina or giddiness due to low Blood Pressure.
— Altered Bowel habits constipation or diarrhoea.
— Attacks of pneumonia or urinary infections.

All these problems can be controlled by keeping Blood Sugar under control by proper diet and by regular exercise.

— They should attend Diabetes education camps and should monitor their Diabetes control by getting Blood Sugar or urine sugar examination once or twice weekly.
— Regular exercise 30 to 45 minute walk will not only help in controlling Diabetes but also helps in controlling weight and high blood pressure.

— Diet schedule should be planned. Avoid missing meals or undue exercise which could lead to hypoglycaemia.

— Avoid taking Extra dose of medicine if you have forgotten in the morning as it may cause hypolycaemia (Low Blood Sugar).

— Whenever there is any evidence of cough or chest infection or urinary infection contact your doctor.

— People whose movements are restricted due to arthritis can perform other types of exercises like stretching of arms or limbs to avoid stiffness of joints.

— Constipation or loose motions can be the complications of diabetes so avoid use of strong laxatives. Control of Blood Sugar and use of fiber in diet like ISABGOL HUSK with water, would help in relieving constipation.

Diabetes in Children

A. Childhood Diabetes

Initially, for two to three years, child looks normal but as he grows old, he gets more prone to infections. Usually child is hospitalized for some chest or other infections and investigations will reveal that child is having high Blood Sugar levels called as IDDM.

In school, child may go for frequent urination or may not be able to see Black Board clearly or if he was very active in studies or in sports earlier, now feels lazy or tired, all these symptoms are suggestive of Diabetes. He should be investigated for Diabetes. Diabetes in children is different than from that of adults as they would need Insulin injections regularly. Junk food, chocolates, ice creams, and cold drinks have to be avoided.

B. Treatment

* Daily Insulin injection
* Diet
* Exercise

Insulin

Children are taught to take injections themselves and Blood Sugar should be monitored regularly to adjust the dose of Insulin.

Tablets are not effective and should not be given to Diabetic children.

Diet

A Diabetic child should eat small frequent meals to prevent fluctuations of the Blood Sugar.

Total calories in diet are calculated on the basis of child's age and body weight. Diet would very as per child's activity. They can have frequent meals instead of one or two big meals.

Exercise

Exercise is important for a diabetic child but, it should be avoided immediately after injection.

Diabetes-Picnic-cum-Education camps are helpful where team of Doctors, Dieticians, Diabetes educators can discuss openly with children and their parents about treatment and other problems.

Counselling of parents to over come the emotional outburst of Diabetic Children is one of the important aspect of Diabetes Management.

Unrecognized Hypoglycemia

Low blood glucose is called hypoglycemia. When you have low blood glucose but don't feel the usual symptoms, it is called unrecognized hypoglycemia (or hypoglycemia unawareness).

If you take insulin or certain diabetes pills, your blood glucose can go too low. For people with diabetes, this is usually defined as blood glucose below 70 mg/dL.

Usually, a person feels symptoms of hypoglycemia such as light headedness, palpitation or shakiness. However, nerve damage (neuropathy) can affect your body's reaction to low blood glucose. Also, if you have hypoglycemia often, you may get used to how it feels and not realize when you are going too low.

If you don't realize your blood glucose is low, you may not be able to treat it easily or on your own. Before you realize it, you may have severe hypoglycemia, which means you will need help from others to treat it. At that stage, you might even have a seizure or lose consciousness. If you are driving a car or using machinery, you could put yourself and others in danger.

Symptoms

There is a range of symptoms for low blood glucose. If you have unrecognized hypoglycemia or hypoglycemia unawareness, you may not have any early symptoms at all. Those around you may notice the signs of your low blood glucose. Following are the range of symptoms that may occur.

Early Symptoms

These usual symptoms of low blood glucose are usually absent when you have unrecognized hypoglycemia.

- Shakiness
- Weakness
- Irritability or nervousness
- Cold, clammy skin
- Paleness
- Hunger
- Light-headedness or dizziness
- Rapid heart beat

Advanced Symptoms

Often, these are the first symptoms you or those around you might notice when you have unrecognized hypoglycemia.

- Lack of coordination

- Slow or slurred speech
- Difficulity in concentrating
- Slowed thinking
- Sudden mood or behaviour changes

Overnight Symptoms

You might not notice these symptoms, but someone who is with you might notice. Low blood glucose during sleep can become severe.

- Sweating
- Crying out in sleep
- Having nightmares
- Tossing and turning
- Waking up confused

Treating Lows

If you experience any of the symptoms, you need to test your blood glucose and follow Routine 15 to 70 to treat Low as needed.

Routine 15 to treat lows

- When you feel symptoms of a low, do a self-test of blood glucose.
- If your number is too low, eat or drink 15 grams of carbohydrate.
- Wait 15 minutes. Do another self-test.
- If your number is still too low, eat or drink another 15 grams of carbohydrate.
- Wait 15 minutes, Test again. If necessary, eat or drink another 15 grams of carbohydrate.
- If your blood glucose remains too low after three treatments, call your provider or physician.

* Some carbohydrate choices are 3-4 glucose tablets, ½ cup juice, or ½ cup regular soft drink (not diet).

If symptoms are not treated with carbohydrate, you may have a seizure or lose consciousness. In case of a severe low, keep an up-to-date prescription glucagon kit on hand. Glucagon is a hormone that raises blood glucose. Your family, friends, and coworkers need to be trained to administer glucagon. Remind them not to inject insulin or give you anything by mouth if you are unconscious. Instruct them to call your doctor/diabetologist if treatment does not work.

Working with Your Provider

Tell your provider if you:

- Notice any changes in your usual warning symptoms of hypoglycemia
- Are having low blood glucose levels without warning or more often than usual
- Have had severe episodes of hypoglycemia

Ask your provider how often to test your blood glucose. Also, ask at what blood glucose level you should treat lows. The usual target (less than 70 mg/dL) may not be best for everyone. Your target might be higher to help you avoid severe lows. Adjusting your blood glucose target for a short time is another option. This often improves your ability to sense hypoglycemia symptoms.

Work with your diabetes care team to adjust your food and activity plan. This can also help reduce episodes of hypoglycemia.

Your provider may also review your insulin plan and adjust your doses or suggest a new type of insulin. Another possibility, in some cases, is an insulin pump. A pump delivers insulin steadily and may reduce your risk for hypoglycemia.

Diabetes Care Schedule

To prevent complications, you need to follow the care schedule below.

Care Item	*Frequency*	*Traget*
A1C	Every 3mos.	Under 7%
Blood pressure	Every visit	Under 120/80 mmHg
LDL cholesterol*	Yearly	Under 100 mgm/dl (With heart disease: under 70 mg/dl)
HDL cholesterol	Yearly	Over 40 mg/dl
Triglycerides	Yearly	Under 150 mg/dl
Albumin/ creatinine ratio (urine protein)	Yearly	Under 30mg/g Cr
Visual foot exam	Every 3 mos.	Normal
Complete Foot exam	Yearly	Normal
Retinal eye exam	Yearly	Normal
Dental exam	Every 6 mos	Normal
Tobacco use	Every visit	No tobacco use
Body mass index(BMI)	Every visit	Under 25
Waist Circumference	Every3-6 months	Women: Under 80 cms Men: 90 cms.
Treatment plan Review	Every 3mos	Completed
Diabetes education	Yearly	Completed

- If you are taking medication to lower your LDL, a drop of at least 30% is best to help reduce your risk of heart disease-no matter what your LDL level is.

About Diabetes Complication

Diabetes can lead to other health problems.

These are called diabetes complications.

Studies show that taking care of your diabetes can help prevent complications. You can also take action to keep them from getting worse.

Complications start with damage to the body's blood vessel and nerves. High blood glucose (Sugar) levels over time can cause this damage. High blood pressure and abnormal cholesterol levels also play key roles. Damaged blood vessels and nerves affect the body's organs and systems.

Other diabetes complications are:

- Depression
- Digestive and urine problems
- Eye disease
- Foot and sensory (nerve) problems
- Heart and blood vessel disease
- Kidney disease
- Oral health problems
- Pregnancy-related problems
- Sexual dysfunction

Ask your provider about your risks and what you can do to prevent, delay, or treat complications.

Actions you Can Take

If you have unrecognized hypoglycemia, test your blood glucose often. If you are low, follow *Routine* 15 *to Treat Lows* as given in previous page. If you think you may be low but are unable to test, eat or drink something with carbohydrate. Test when you get a chance.

Keep careful records of your blood glucose tests, food eaten, activity, and changes in your insulin doses. Whenever you are low, review your records and try to figure out what might have caused it. Share this information with your provider. These records can help you both spot patterns of lows caused by exercise or other changes in your daily routine.

Be alert for new warning signs of low blood glucose. Share any new information with your provider, relatives, and friends. Give your family and friends periodic refreshers on how to recognize and treat your lows.

You also need to:

- Test before bed, between 1 am. and 3 a.m., and first thing in the morning if you suspect you are having lows overnight.
- Test before you drive and every couple of hours during a long trip.
- Keep a few sources of carbohydrate with you, especially in your car.
- Always wear or carry Medical I.D.

Monitoring of Diabetes

Why and How to Control?

What is Meant by Good Control?

1. Normal blood sugar levels 70 mg%-140mg%
   Acceptable for diabetics 90mg%, 180mg%
   Ideal 60-100mg% fasting, 140 mg% to 160mg% 2hrs after meals.
2. Weight—as near to ideal as possible.
3. Blood pressure normal.
4. Blood fats (Cholesterol and triglycerides) normal.
5. Glycosylated Haemoglobin levels normal.

How do you know you have good control?

By regular testing of :

(1) **Blood Sugar**	(2) **Urine Sugar**	(3) **Urine Ketones**
Direct reading	Indirect guide: results depend on (a) blood sugar level (b) renal threshold	Ketones are acid substances produced from excessive break-down of stored fats
↓	↓	↓
Shows low, normal and high blood sugars	An indication of blood sugar levels	They may occur: (a) When not enough insulin (b) when losing weight (c) Following hypo
↓	↓	↓

When to Test

Blood Sugar / Urine Sugar	Urine Ketones
If on insulin : before each meal and before bed or as directed If not on insulin : before breakfast and 2 hrs after meals or as directed	Each morning and more frequently when: (a) sick or (b) when Blood Sugar level is 260 mg% 100 ml

Also check regularly:

1. Weight.
2. Blood fats.
3. Glycosylated Heamoglobin.
4. Blood Pressure.

Why aim for good control?

1. To avoid complications:
   (a) Short-term.
   (b) Long-term affecting.
2. To lead as normal lifestyle as possible.
3. For general good health and feeling well.

How do you achieve good control?

1. Stick to your diet.
2. Get plenty of exercise.
3. Make sure your techniques are accurate.

Come to a Diabetes education programme:

4. If all these things are OK and you still have poor control than see your doctor to review your medication.

Good control of Diabetes and preventing long-term complications:

1. Diabetes may slowly damage some parts of your body. This damage can impair the quality and longevity of your life.
2. Certain factors may lead to the development of these complications. These are called: Risk Factors.
3. Nor everyone who has diabetes will develop complications.
4. The presence of one or more of these risk factors may increase your chance of developing the complications that are associated with diabetes.

What are the Risk Factors?

1. Poor control of Blood Sugar—Over an extended period of time.
2. Smoking—Can affect blood vessels.
3. High Blood fat levels—Can lead to damage of blood vessels.
4. High blood pressure—Can damage arteries and kidneys.

Lack of knowledge

Early warning signs may be missed. Education and early treatment my help to lesson damage.

Damage

Blood vessels		*Nerves*	
Large may cause build up of deposits in the vessels which can cause the blockages.	Small may cause weakness in the vessel—wall causing them to break and bleed.	Autonomic low or no response or action from the nerves controlled automatically.	Peripheral decreased sensation from the nerves to the brain.

Summary

You can decrease your risks by:

— Maintaining good control of Blood Sugar level.
— Maintaining ideal weight.
— Participating in regular exercise.
— Take medication as prescribed.
— Stop smoking.
— Participate in diabetes education programmes.

Facts/Views of Diabetic Patients About their Disease

1. Diabetes is a common disease does not require any special treatment except reduction of sugar in food/sweet items.
2. Only 25 to 30 per cent of diabetic patients take regular treatment.
3. Diabetic patient consult their doctor when there is some problem like cuts at private parts (penis) or itching or for some other complications of diabetes.
4. Only 10 to 20 per cent of diabetics get their Blood Sugar tested regularly. Majority of diabetic patients don't get their Blood Sugar tested for months together.
5. Very few diabetic patients are careful about their weight and diet control.
6. Most of the diabetic patients are eager to switch on to some magic pill after the control of their diabetes and would stop regular medicines. After few months when they go for Blood Sugar checkup they are shocked to see their very high Blood Sugar levels.
7. Diabetic patients would try to hide their reports and are not interested in discussing their problem with others.
8. Most of the diabetic patients would prefer to change the doctor who advises them to use Insulin for Blood Sugar control. They would go on changing doctors and would waste lot of time. Their reasons for refusing Insulin injections are :

    - This will make a habit.
    - Disease has reached at its peak.
    - Insulin damages body organs.

Alcohol And Diabetes

For Diabetics, is it safe to Drink?

Alcohol is everywhere—when the family gathers, at parties. "What will you have?" Some one asks. If you have diabetes, what do you say?

It all depends. Start by asking yourself three basic questions:

- — Is my diabetes under control?
- — Does my doctor agree that I am free from health problems that alcohol can make worse (like nerve damage or High B.P.) that alcohol can make worse.
- — Do I know how alcohol can affect me and my diabetes?

If you said "yes" to all three, it's okay to have an occasional drink. What does occasional mean? The American Diabetes Association suggests that you have no more than two drinks a day.

Your Body and Alcohol

Alcohol moves very quickly into the blood without being broken down (metabolized) in your stomach. Within five minutes of having a drink, there is enough alcohol in your blood to measure. Thirty to ninety minutes after having drink, the alcohol in your bloodstream is at its highest level.

Your liver does most of the job of breaking down the alcohol once it is in your body. But it needs time. If your weight is 70 kg., it will take about 2 hours to metabolize a beer or mixed drink.

If you drink alcohol faster than your liver can break it down, the excess alcohol moves through your bloodstream to other parts of your body. Brain cells are easy targets. When someone talks about getting a buzz from alcohol, this is what they are feeling.

Risks of Low Blood Glucose

If you have diabetes and take Insulin shots or oral diabetes pills, you risk low blood glucose when you drink alcohol. To protect yourself, never drink on an empty stomach. Plan to have your drink with a meal or after eating a snack that contains protein, fat or both.

How does alcohol add to your chances of having low blood glucose? It has to do with your liver.

Normally, when your blood glucose level starts to drop, your liver steps in. It goes to work changing stored carbohydrate into glucose. Then it sends the glucose out into the blood, which helps you avoid or slow down a low blood glucose reaction.

However, when alcohol enters your system, this changes. Alcohol is a toxin. Your body reacts to alcohol like a poison. The liver, wants to clear it from the blood quickly. In fact, the liver won't put out glucose again until it has taken care of the alcohol. If your blood glucose level is falling, you can quickly wind up with very low blood glucose.

This is why drinking as little as 2 ounces of alcohol (about 2 drinks) on an empty stomach can lead to very low blood glucose.

When you mix alcohol and exercise, you increase the risk of going low. This can happen because exercise helps lower your blood glucose levels. Let's say you've just played a couple of hard sets of tennis. You have a beer after the match. But in the hours after the game, your body is still working. It replaces the energy your muscles used up. To do this, it clears glucose from the blood and adds it to the muscles's store. This is why hard exercise can cause your blood glucose level to go down.

If you take Insulin or diabetes pills, they too are working to clear glucose from your blood. Unless you eat or your liver adds glucose to your blood, you could be heading for a very low blood glucose level. If you drink a beer, the alcohol will stop your liver from sending out any glucose. Your chances of going low are even greater.

If you take diabetes pills that work over a long period of time, such as chlorpropamide diabetese, you are at risk for very low blood glucose when drinking. This is because alcohol changes how the diabetes pill works. It makes the pill stronger and longer lasting. Hopefully, your doctor warned you about mixing long lasting diabetes pill with alcohol.

Low blood glucose when drinking is less of a risk for those with Type II diabetes who control their diabetes by diet and exercise alone.

Don't Go Low

Following these guidelines to avoid low blood glucose levels when you drink:

— Never drink alcohol on an empty stomach.
— Limit yourself to 1 or 2 drinks.

If you just finished hard exercise, test your blood glucose before you drink and at least once, while you're drinking. Watch for falling blood glucose levels in the hours after exercise.

Alcohol also effects your body's ability to get over a low blood glucose level. If you have low blood glucose, you may need to treat it more than once as time goes by. If you have been drinking, check your blood glucose before you go to sleep. You may need to have a snack before you retire to avoid a low blood glucose reaction while you sleep.

Heavy drinking over time can hurt your liver. It won't be able to make glucose as well. When this happens, your diabetes is harder to control.

Alcoholic drinks can have anywhere from 60 to 300 calories each.

To Decrease the Calories

- Put less liquor in your drink.
- Choose light beer over regular beer.
- Use dry wine.

Diabetes and Smoking

Quitting smoking is good for your diabetes and also is good for your health. When you quit smoking, you lower your blood glucose and blood pressure. You lower your total cholesterol, LDL cholesterol (the bad kind), and your triglycerides. When you quit smoking, you raise your HDL cholesterol (the good kind) and your oxygen intake. You even raise your life expectancy!

Quit smoking and you can reduce your risk for heart disease, blood vessel disease, kidney disease, nerve disease, dental disease, and cancer (mouth, throat, lungs, and bladder). You can reduce your risk of heart attack and stroke, miscarriage or stillbirth, limited joint mobility, and colds, bronchitis, and emphysema.

Quit smoking and you can even reduce your risk for insulin resistance (when your body does not respond to insulin). No wonder people try to quit. Here are some helpful hints.

Before you Quit

- Write down each time you smoke for a week. Write down any event or activity you were doing or about to do. Save the list.
- Write down all these reasons you want to quit. Read the list each day of the week before you quit.
- Pick a day to quit and write it down. Choose a day with few pressures. That way, stress won't tempt you to smoke. You may want to do it when you've got some time off from work.
- Tell others you plan to quit. Let family, friends, and co-workers know. Seek their support. Tell them how they can help you. For example, ask them not to offer you a cigarette. Tell them what to expect when you first quit.

- Choose a method of quitting. There are many ways to quit smoking. Not every method work for every person. Your diabetes-care team may be able to help you find a method that will work for you. It might be using a nicotine patch or chewing gum. Hyposis helps some peoples stop smoking. For other, acupuncture stops the craving to smoke.
- If you would find it easier to quit with other people, think about joining a stop-smoking class.
- Practice deep breathing. Relaxation tapes may help.
- Stock up on raw vegetables and other low-fat, low-calorie snacks. Your appetite may increase after you quit smoking. You may gain weight (the average gain is 7 pounds). You may crave sweet foods.
- Begin to exercise a few weeks before you quit smoking. More activity will help you combat withdrawal symptoms and weight gain. Exercise can take the place of smoking or help you control the urge to eat. Try brisk walking, cycling, or swimming.
- Plan rewards for not smoking. For example, you might play a favourite game one week, go to a movie the next week.

After you Quit

The first 3 months or so after quitting are the hardest. Most people who return to smoking do so then. Try these tactics for staying smoke-free.

- Refer to the list you make of events or activities that were going on around the time you smoked. The next time and of those events or activities comes up, avoid it. For example, if you always smoke at happy hour, don't go.
- If you can't avoid the event, replace the cigarette with something else. Hold something else in your hand. Try a strand a beads, a polished stone, or a pen. Put something else in your mouth, alike a toothpick. Chew gum or ice.

- If you smoke to relax, find another way to relax. Try deep breathing or relaxation exercises. If you smoke to perk up, try to walk or stretching.
- Throw away your cigarettes, butts, lighters, matches, and ash-trays.
- Put your list or reasons for quitting where you had kept your cigarettes.
- Read your list of reasons for quitting. Remind yourself that you did not want to smoke.
- Remind yourself that all it takes is one cigarette to become a smoker again. Try to avoid even one.
- Make a list of things you like about not smoking.
- If you are worried about gaining weight, talk with your dietitian about changing your meal and exercise plans.

Vacations, Travel and Diabetes

Introduction

There is no reason for you to avoid travel just because you have diabetes. With a few extra precautions, you can take as many vacations to as many places as your imagination can suggest. A little planning and common sense are all that's required.

General Do's and Don'ts

Do carry extra medicine supplies with you—enough to last longer than you plan to be away. That way, if you decide to extend the trip or if you are delayed, you won't have to worry about finding the supplies you need. A good rule of thumbs is to carry twice the supplies you normally need for trips of a week or less, and one week extra for longer trips.

You'll need your insulin, syringes, swabs, blood testing and urine testing equipment, some form of identification stating that you have diabetes and what your medications and dosages are. Carry extra food in case meals are delayed or missed, Don't pack these supplies in your luggage which is checked. It is safer to pack your supplies in a carry-on case.

Also Carry

- A letter and prescription from your doctor for your insulin and syringes.
- Motion sickness pills.
- Medicine to relieve possible vomiting or diarrhoea.
- Sugar cubes, dried fruit or long acting carbohydrate.
- See your doctor before you go get extra supplies of medicines.

Travelling by Car

Auto trips can be very enjoyable. But a long drive could leave you miles from available food at your scheduled meal times, so bring along a snack to sandwich enough to fill the needs of your individual meal plan. Then, even if you have car trouble, you won't take the chance of missing a meal.

If you're doing the driving be sure you have about 15 grams of carbohydrate every hour to guard against low blood sugar and a possible Insulin reaction which could affect your driving ability. A small piece of fruit such as a peach, pear, apple or orange, two large sugar cubes, a small box of raisins, or two crackers will provide about the right amount of carbohydrate. Also, don't forget the importance of blood testing during the trip to keep a close watch on blood glucose levels.

Don't keep your Insulin anywhere in the car where it could become very hot or cold, such as the dashboard or boot. Extreme temperatures can change your insulin's effectiveness. A good rule of thumb: if the temperature is comfortable for you, it is a safe temperature for your Insulin.

Buses and Trains

When you travel by bus or train, rest stops and meal times may not match your schedule. And there can be unexpected delays. Carry a snack such as packaged cheese and crackers, or a sandwich, or a piece of fruit, so that you can provide your body with the sugar it needs at your regular meal-time. And, of course, carry your insulin, syringes, and diabetes identifications with you, rather than leaving those things with your luggage. If you're travelling alone, it's a good idea to let the driver or conductor know that you have diabetes, just in case you should have a problem.

In flight Injections

On a long flight, you may be scheduled for an injection while you're in the air. Follow your normal procedure with one difference put only one half as much air into your Insulin bottle as you normally would. Cabin pressure in high-altitude flight is lower than pressure on the ground, so you won't need as much pressure inside the bottle to balance the Insulin you draw.

Carry a Sugar Source

You should always carry some form of sugar that can be eaten easily. This could be food such as raisins, sugar cubes or a piece of fresh fruit. Any of these sources can give you enough sugar to help you avoid a low blood sugar reaction (also called an "Insulin reaction" or "hypoglycaemia").

When you are travelling chances are your routine will be different from when you are at home, and the risks of a reaction are greater. Even people who normally are very aware of the signs of a reaction, can be caught off guard by the stress and excitement of travel.

Your doctor may suggest one of the instant glucose preparations. These are designed to be given by mouth, and to get sugar into your bloodstream quickly in case of emergency. If your doctor does suggest one of these preparations, make sure that someone you're travelling with understands how to use it.

Blood Testing is a Must

The excitement and stress of a vacation, the changes in your daily routine, meal timing, and the kinds of food available can all affect your blood sugar levels. Test your blood for sugar at least few times.

Are You Losing Weight

One has to keep the weight under control for proper Diabetes Management. If persons is over weight/obese he develops Insulin resistance. *Efficacy* of Insulins actions on tissues is reduced and Diabetes becomes uncontrolled. Sometimes Diabetic patients go on losing weight inspite of regular treatment. The reasons may be:

1. Either you are taking very low calories diet in place of diet advised to you by your doctor (say you are advised to take 1800 calories diet but you are taking 1200 calories diet).
2. Whenever sugar levels are very high and diabetes is uncontrolled one is passing sugar with urine. For Energy sugar is not available, it uses available sugar in body and thereby causing weight loss.
3. When patient is using medicines like Metformin, Glyciphage or Glycomet etc. These medicines reduce appetite and reduce weight.
4. If there are associated diseases like Tuberculosis, Thyroid disease *or* patient is having loose motions or vomiting.

Treatment

If even with balanced diet patient is losing weight then it is matter of concern and he/she should consult doctor.

— Have proper calories diet! consult dietician/doctor.
— Don't adjust/change medicines yourself.
— If your doctor advises you to take Insulin Don't Resist.

It will stop weight loss and would control Blood Sugar.

Diabetes Prevention and High Risk Group to Develop Diabetes

Incidence of diabetes is increasing more and more, new cases are detected everyday due to public awareness, at the same time everyone ask this question: How we can prevent Diabetes and its complications?

One thing is sure that NIDDM can be prevented, its onset can be delayed and one can even prevent complications to great extent.

Change in lifestyle, food habits and sedentary habits have contributed to this increase in the incidence of Diabetes.

Type I/IDDM—Disease presents in childhood, islet cell antibodies and insulin auto-antibodies are present at the age of 2 years—By some virus infection or other factors cause activation of Immune response—this in turn destroy Beta-cells of pancrease.

Screening can be done by analysing genetic factors and Immune measures marriage between two diabetics should be avoided.

In NIDDM/Type II

It takes about 10-15 years to develop symptoms of diabetes. During this period initially there is impaired Glucose tolerance test then abnormal glucose tolerance test and finally Symptomatic diabetes. As this problem is seen in relatives of NIDDM, thorough screening of family members for impaired/Abnormal glucose tolerance test can detect potential future diabetic patients. Regular exercise, weight reduction and diet control can stop the progression of disease and delay the symptoms for many years. Antioxidants should be taken regularly.

Marriage of two diabetics should be avoided.

Diabetes and Depression

Major depressive disorder is present in 15 to 20 per cent of patients with diabetes. Even after successful treatment depression will return in 80 per cent of diabetic patients.

Depression in diabetes has a special relevance, as depression has association with poor compliance with diabetic treatment, poor glycaemic control and increased risk for micro and macrovascular complications.

One hundred and eighty-eight patients of Type II diabetes (aged 40-47 years) were studied for symptoms and well being in relation to glycaemic control.

Higher HbA_{1c} levels were significantly associated with higher symptoms scores (Total score hyperglycaemic and neuropathic score) with worse mood (total score, displeasure score, depression, tension, fatigue) and the worse general well being.

The data suggested that better glycaemic control in Type II diabetes is associated with fewer physical symptoms, better mood and better well being in non-hypoglycaemic HbA_{1c} range.

"Diabetes is associated with increased risk of psychological disturbance especially for those with more diabetes related complications."

Insulin dependent diabetic patients who reported feeling depressed, anxious or stressed out were among least likely to successfully lower their Blood Sugar Levels, even after learning to practice relaxation techniques.

Aspirin for Diabetics

Diabetics have as 2-4 fold increase in the risk of dying from the complications of heart diseases.

American Diabetes Association recommends use of Aspirin for both primary prevention and secondary prevention.

Primary Prevention

Use of Aspirin in High Risk people with diabetes would prevent them from heart attacks and stroke.

Risk Factors in Type I and II Diabetes are:

- A Family History of Heart Attacks
- Cigarette Smoking
- Hypertension
- Obesity
- Albminuria
- People with High Cholesterol and Triglyceride levels
- Those who are above 30 years

All these people can take tablet of Aspirin as per recommendation of their doctor. You must consult your Doctor before using Aspirin.

Always take Aspirin after Food.

Use of Aspirin for Secondary Prevention

Your Doctor would recommend you to take Aspirin if you have evidence of large vessel disease, i.e.,

(i) After Heart attack (Acute MI)

(ii) After By-pass Surgery
(iii) After Stroke
(iv) Evidence of having blockage of Arteries of legs
(v) Those who have ANGINA.

Therefore use of Aspirin is recommended for both, i.e.

(i) Those who are going to develop complications,
(ii) Those who already have evidence of complications and to prevent further recurrence.

Are You in High Risk Group for Diabetes

Please reply all Questions

1.	Are you overweight? (this obesity is Apple Type)	Yes/No.
2.	Are you Leading Sedentry Lifestyle. (No Exercise)?	Yes/No.
3.	Do you have Family History of Diabetes?	Yes/No.
4.	Are you over 40 years of Age?	Yes/No.
5.	Did you have Diabetes during Pregnancy?	Yes/No.
6.	Do you suffer from High Blood Pressure?	Yes/No.
7.	Do you have High Blood Cholesterol and Triglycerides in your Blood?	Yes/No.

If your answer is yes to any of the above question, you are in a high risk group for development of Diabetes.

Diabetes can be prevented

If you are in high risk group get Glucose Tolerance Test (G.T.T.). If it is Abnormal then control your diet, reduce weight by regular exercise. You can prevent diabetes by these means.

> People who carry more weight on the hips and thighs are pear-shaped. People who carry more weight around the waist and abdomen are apple-shaped. Apple-shaped people are more likely to have blood vessel disease, heart disease, high blood pressure, high blood fat levels, insulin resistance and poor blood glucose control.

My Story of Diabetes

Hypoglycaemic Story

Mrs. Goel aged 40 years was brought to hospital emergency at 6 a.m., she was unconscious at that time. Relatives gave the history that she is a Diabetic patient and was on Insulin injections. Her hand and feet were cold and clothes were wet. She had headache in the morning and disturbed sleep. Her Blood Sugar was 45 mg/100ml. She was given I.V. glucose in hospital and within 1/2 an hour started recovering. She recovered completely after 4 hours. According to her she missed her evening meals after Insulin injection in morning (long acting). This was Hypoglycaemic Coma and this occurs due to sudden decrease in Blood Sugar after Insulin or tablets. After tablets, specially, this low Blood Sugar state can last up to 72 years.

Second Story

Till 1976 I was alright, then I started having cuts and itching around penis. I consulted doctor who advised Blood Sugar testing which revealed Diabetes. I was advised to take certain pills and in this way 16 years passed.

In 1992, I sustained some injury to feet and was showing to my General Physician who would do dressing of wound. One day I noticed black colour at the injury site and showed it to Diabetologist. It was gangrene of great toe and my toe was (amputated) removed. I was able to walk again.

In between I used to have chest discomfort and high blood pressure and was taking medicines for it too.

In 1992 December as soon as finished my dinner, some labourers who were working in home called me from down stairs.

I immediately started coming down but on the way I felt short of breath and suffocation in chest. I was shifted to hospital and to my surprise it was heart attack, not a gas discomfort or indigestion which I was thinking. Now I have undergone By-pass Surgery and on regular Insulin injections.

IDDIM Story

I am 13 year old boy and taking Insulin injections regularly.

I was alright till the age of 9 years and then had viral fever. I was diagnosed having Pneumonia and at the same time having diabetes. No one was ready to accept it, they attributed it to antibiotics or treatment. Before this attack I used to feel weakness I would feel extreme weakness and sleepy but my parents thought that this was due to my excessive play and physical activities. Finally, I landed in hospital both with chest infection and at that time I was diagnosed having Diabetes which would require regular Insulin injections.

Now I take injection twice daily and feel like any other child except having daily pricks.

My Experience

I am a Diabetic child. When I returned from the hospital 3 years-back, it was very difficult for my relatives or society to accept that I am a Diabetic. They considered Diabetes is a curse. (मधुमेह एक अभिशाप है।) I would have felt very sad that I am not a normal child, but my family gave me strength to fight with Diabetes. I accepted Diabetes in my life as a challenge. I want to give an assurance to society that I am like a normal child. I can do everything what a non-Diabetic do. Only I have to take some precautions. Even Diabetic person can live healthy life as a normal person. Why our society considered Diabetes a problem? They considered taking injections twice a day is a very big problem. We eat food, drink water, go to school, board bus, drive car/scooter and do many scores of other activities. Even we breath every second. Do we consider all these activities as a problem?

Friends, let us take a pledge and consider ourselves not a symbol of sympathy and should not avail of any special privileged offered. Behave like a normal child and do all that is expected of a normal child. Someone has rightly said that—

Diabetic Life is a challenge	Meet it
Diabetic Life is a Struggle	Accept it
Diabetic Life is a Battle	Fight it
Diabetic Life is a Problem	Solve it
Diabetic Life is a Sorrow	Overcome it
Diabetic Life is a Game	Play it

—Bhawna Chawla, XII Class (16 years)

Hall leads Hopes in 100ml Freestyle

Gary Hall will try to give the USA the lift it needs in the 100-metre freestyle in the Sydney Olympics. (News)

Hall, 25, saved the USA from its first loss in Olympics history in the 4 × 100 freestyle relay at the 1996 Atlanta Game. Swimming the anchor leg, he produced what was then the fastest relay split ever (47.45 seconds) and brought the USA from third to first, winning in a Olympic record of 3.15.41 minutes. He also won silver in the individual 100, just 0.26 seconds behind Alexander Popov of Russia.

Hall was diagnosed with diabetes, and he thought his career was over. He learned to manage his diabetes by constantly monitoring his Blood Sugar, balancing his energy expenditure with his eating and taking appropriate medication.

The thing is every time he wins a race, it is a victory against diabetes—a hope for millions of sufferers wanting to lead not just normal but winning lives.

Foot Care in Diabetes

As the sensations of pain and temperature are diminished in feet due to involvement of nerves in diabetes, one should be very careful. If there is some cut or ulcer due to shoe bite, diabetic patient will notice it very late.

Each day, set aside a regular time (such as after bathing) to inspect your feet. Check between your toes as well as all the sides for blisters, cuts, scratches, cracks, corns, and calluses. Examine the balls of your feet for dryness and broken skin. During examination, look or feel for warts and ingrowing toe nails.

If you notice anything unusual—particularly sores, redness, or infection—see your doctor at once.

Foot Care Do's

* Keep feet clean, warm and dry.
* Wash (Don't soak) feet daily with warm (not hot) water.
* Use mild hand soap; rinse well.
* Dry feet thoroughly, especially, between toes.
* Powder feet and shoes after bathing.
* Use mild lubricating lotion in small amounts and massage well (between toes).
* Trim toe nails straight across; file with emery board.
* Wear comfortable, well-fitting shoes (leather is best).
* Break in new shoes gradually.
* Inspect shoes for objects, torn lining, rough spots which can injure feet.
* Wear clean socks everyday.
* Check socks or stockings for pus or unusual odour.
* Wear loose-fitting socks to bed if needed to protect from cold.

For proper foot care, what you don't do is sometimes just as important as what you do. Here are some general "to-dos" that, with daily attention, will become second nature.

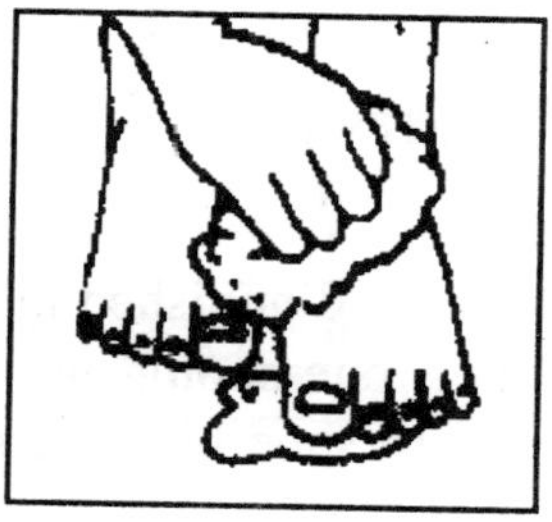

Wash feet with water and soap

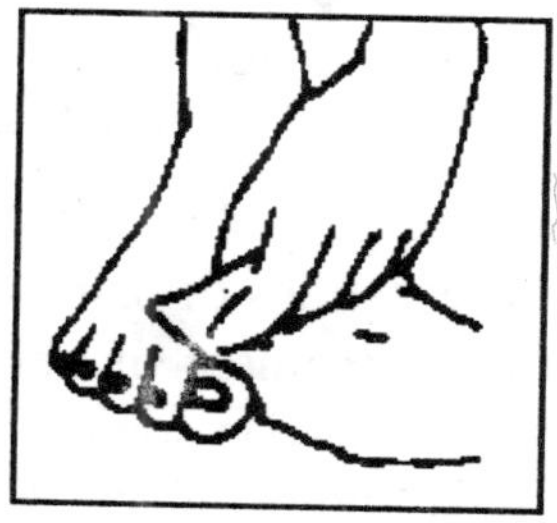

Clean the area between two toes

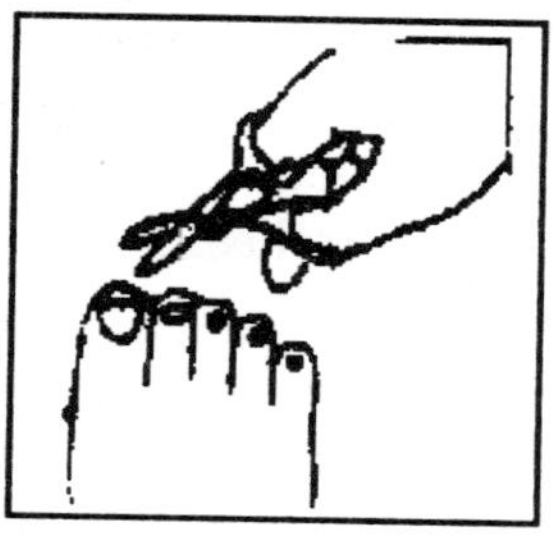

Cut nails properly

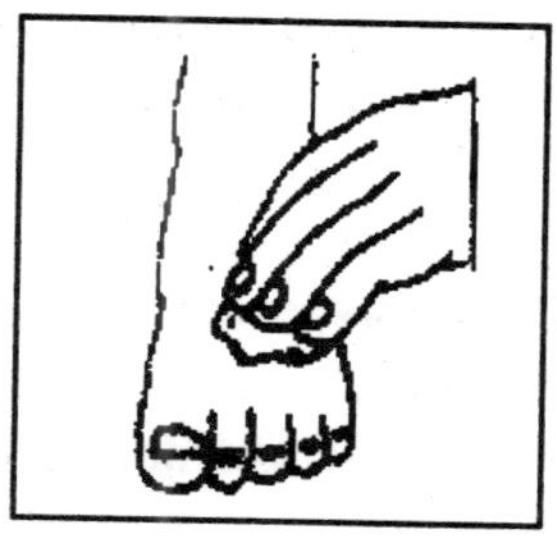

Use moisturizer for skin

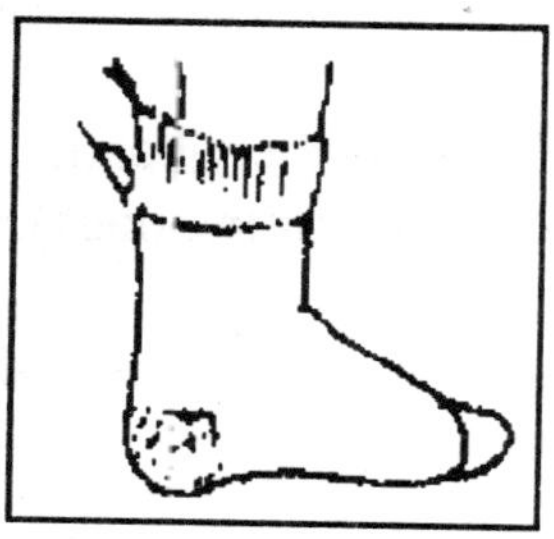

Use clean and proper size socks and stockings

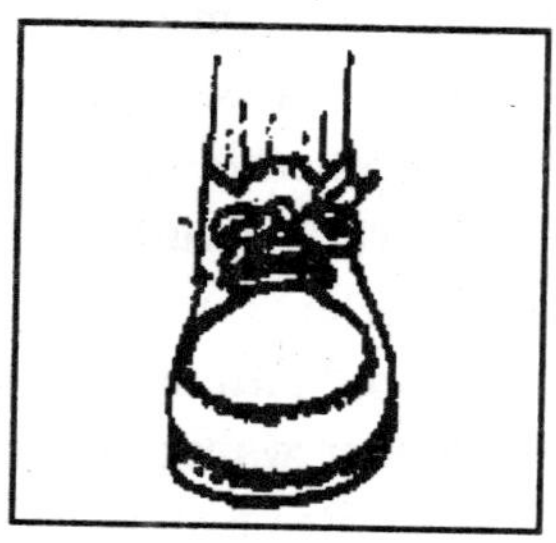

Keep your foot dry and warm

Don't walk bare footed in home or outside

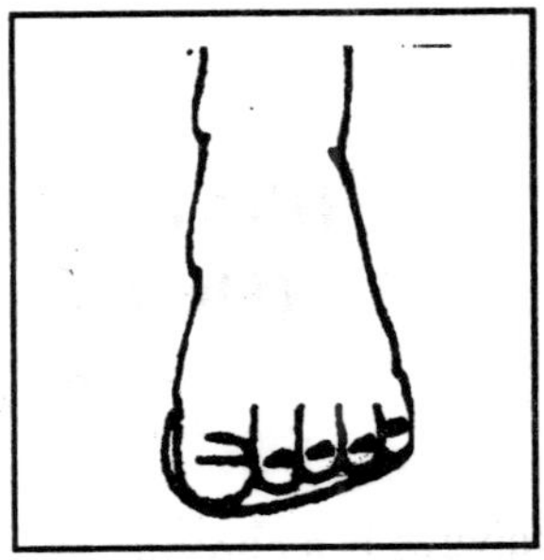

Use proper size shoes

Foot Care Don'ts

* Avoid exposure of feet to extremes of hot and cold.
* Never keep feet too moist or too dry.
* Don't pull off or cut loose pieces of skin.
* Never cut thick toe nails, corns, or calluses. Rely on a foot specialist.
* Avoid chemicals for corns or callus removal.
* Don't use hot foot soaks, heating pads, or hot-water bottles.
* Don't use perfumed lotions.
* Don't use adhesive tape on skin.
* Don't wear shoes without stockings or socks.
* Avoid open-toed shoes.
* Don't wear socks with holes.
* Don't walk barefoot, even indoors.
* Never go without shoes around a swimming pool or hot beach.
* Avoid sitting with legs crossed.
* Never walk on an injured foot.

HbA1c and Mean Blood Glucose (Over a period of 8-10 weeks) and Other Tests

Diabetes is a chronic, yet treatable condition. Recent studies have shown the value of tight blood sugar control in delaying diabetic complications. Good blood sugar control is beneficial for all people with diabetes.

Uncontrolled Diabetes over a period of time leads to following complication:

1. Eye problems
2. Heart Attack
3. Kidney diseases
4. Nerve damage

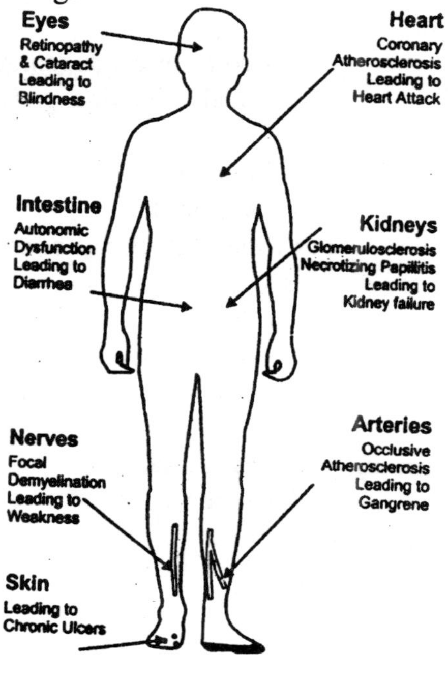

Suggested Investigations

Following investigations should be done to keep a check complications.

Frequency	*Investigations*
Every fortnight	Fasting & PP Glucose (Post Breakfast and Lunch)
Every 3 months	HbA1c and MBG
Every year	Urea, Uric Acid, Creatinine, Lipid Profile, HbA1c and MBG, Micro-albuminuria and Urine Routine

Of these two main tests related to help achieve good blood sugar control are:

1. Blood glucose level monitoring
2. HbA1c and Mean Blood Glucose (MBG)

What is HbA1c?

In the blood stream, sticky glucose attaches to haemoglobin (haemoglobin is the protein in red blood cells that carries oxygen). As the glucose level increases, so does the amount of haemoglobin with glucose riding piggyback. Once glucose attaches to haemoglobin, it stays attached and becomes glychemoglobin- HbA1c.

The HbA1c test tells your doctor about average glucose control over the past 8-10 weeks.

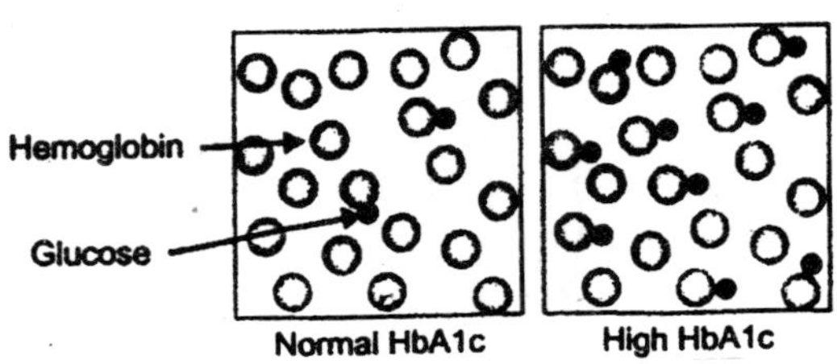

Benefits of HbA1c Testing

By measuring the percentage of HbA1c, doctors can estimate the average glucose level over the life span of the red blood cells. In other words, the HbA1c test reveals long-term control over the last 8-10 weeks.

While blood sugar testing is like a snap shot, HbA1c testing is more like a full-length movie—it provides an overall view of your glucose control.

Reaching Your Target

Your doctor uses your HbA1c results to fine-tune your treatment. The normal range for the HbA1c test is between 4 per cent and 6 per cent. However, people with diabetes may have an HbA1c level greater than 8 per cent. In uncontrolled diabetes, the level may be higher. The ADA recommends that the target for good glucose control is 7 per cent HbA1c.

How often should you be tested for HbA1c?

Getting an HbA1c test is easy. It only requires one sample of blood, drawn at anytime of the day, including right after a meal.

Frequency	*Condition*
Twice a year	If your have stable glucose control and are meeting your treatment targets.
Every 3 Months	If your treatment changes or you are not meeting your targets.

To ensure the best possible care, be sure to ask your doctor for an HbA1c test today. Also, it is important to ensure that your doctor uses a certified HbA1c test. Remember, you'll be looking at the trend in your HbA1c numbers over time, so quality is important.

Using Your HbA1c Test Results

If your HbA1c level is less than 7 per cent you are doing an excellent job of maintaining near normal glucose levels.

If your HbA1c level is greater than 8 per cent, some change in your treatment plan may be needed; check with your doctor.

Achieving your target HbA1c level is the best way to reduce the risk of developing long-term complications.

Get Your Pipes Checked

It is a good idea to get pipes checked. In people with long standing and poorly controlled diabetes, high blood glucose can effect the small blood vessels supplying the kidney and retina and large blood vessels supplying the Brain, Heart and lower limbs (legs and feet). Narrowing of arteries is a normal part of growing old but it is more common in people who have diabetes. Smoking and poor diabetes control make it worse, if you get pain in calf and foot on walking it indicates that the blood supply to the legs is insufficient and that there is obstruction to the blood flow. It can even lead to gangrene which may require amputation of foot or leg.

If you have any of the symptoms listed, check with your doctor to see if you should schedule a painless vascular examination. Early detection of vascular problems can help you to *avoid serious complications and help you enjoy your life to the fullest.*

Current Symptoms:

- Claudication Rt ☐ Lt ☐
  (leg pain during walking which disappears with rest) ☐
- Limb hair loss/Absence ☐
- Skin colour changes ☐
- Trophic Nails ☐
- Numbness, Tingling ☐
- Cold Hands or Feet ☐
- Extermity weakness ☐
- Ulcerations ☐

Care of Kidney in Diabetes

Micral Test (Test for Micro-Albuminurea)

This Test detects microscopic amounts of albumin in the urine and signifies signs of very early kidney damage.

In the early stage of kidney damage, there is a leak of very small amounts of protein (albumin) into the urine. If it is a consistent finding, it indicates that your kidneys have been damaged by your diabetes. If this is the case, then attention to the control of your blood glucose and treatment of high blood pressure is of great importance, as this can stabilize or even reverse the condition.

Test is very simple and for this we only need a sample of urine.

Correlation Between HbA1c and Glucose Levels

HbA_{1c}% Gloucose	Mean Blood mg/dl
4	65
5	100
6	135
7	170
8	205
9	240
10	275
11	310
12	345

Self-Evaluation About Diabetes Control

You read the Questionnaire and judge yourself about:

1. Do you keep records of Blood Glucose Tests or Urine-Tests? **Yes/No**
2. Have you ever adjusted dose of Insulin or Tablets by seeing your records? **Yes/No**
3. At hotels or restaurants you were able to decide the food of your choice according to need of calories prescribed for you? **Yes/No**
4. Have you ever experienced symptoms of hypoglycaemia or low Blood Sugar with your regular exercise programme and again have you adjusted the dose of insulin or oral medicines? **Yes/No**
5. Have you actively participated in the learning process, i.e. group discussions and attending lecture? **Yes/No**
6. Were you able to manage Diabetes during stressful situations, i.e. emotional upset or during some infection etc.? **Yes/No**
7. Have you ever given up treatment schedule, thinking it is futile or useless? **Yes/No**
8. Do you believe that Home Blood glucose monitoring (HBGM) is helpful for better living? **Yes/No**
9. Do you think that sharing the views of diabetics who have lived and coped diabetes for many years, are useful? **Yes/No**
10. Have you ever indulged in excessive drinking knowing that this would have adverse affect on your diabetes control? **Yes/No**

Score

A. If you have score of
   8 Yes
   2 No
   Then you are having excellent understanding of Diabetes and you can manage your Diabetes well.

B. If you have score of
   6 Yes
   4 No
   Although you know about Diabetes, still it needs proper attention to prevent complications of Diabetes.

C. If your score is
   4 Yes or Less
   Then you are having poor control of Diabetes. You are the one who is prone to develop complications of Diabetes. You need proper counselling.

Questions Diabetic Patient Usually Ask

1. Q Whether my disease will be cured or not?

   A Diabetes is a disease which can be controlled by regular exercise, diet control, by oral medicines or by Insulin injections.

2. Q What about sweets and fruits?

   A You can eat fruits and sweets but adjust the food. Say today you want to take one slice of mango, you should not take other fruits on that day.

3. Q Can I substitute extra one tablet for ice-creams or extra diet?

   A No. One should avoid it as it will disturb your diabetes control. Never take medicines along with alcohol.

4. Q If I have forgotten to take Insulin in the morning, can I take double dose in the evening?

   A No. One might go into hypoglycaemia.

5. Q Is it true that heart attack is without pain in diabetics? Then how it is diagnosed?

   A Heart attack is painless or silent. Usually there is no pain; patient gets breathlessness and sinking sensations. E.C.G. helps in diagnosis.

6. Q Is it true that once Insulin is started, it is for ever?

   A If your Blood Sugar levels are very high and not coming under control with medicines, your doctor may advise you to take Insulin. Once Blood Sugar starts coming down then Insulin can be withdrawn.

7. Q Is there any test which one can find out whether kidney's are affected or not?

   A Yes. Kidney's are involved in diabetes invariably. It depends upon duration of diabetes and raised Blood

Sugar Levels. Earliest manifestation is appearances of proteins, called microalbumin in urine. It takes about 5 to 10 years from this stage to reach the final stage of end stage kidney failure. If one keeps Blood Sugar and blood pressure under control at this stage, this process can be reversed.

8. Q Please explain sexual relationship with diabetes control?

A Uncontrolled Diabetes leads to sexual weakness, and impotence and instead of trying sexual stimulants or alcohol one should try to control Blood Sugar. It is true that persistent, high Blood Sugar would worsen the situation. There is urge but you can't perform.

Important Points to Remember

1. If Parents are Diabetic then you have to be careful regarding your weight because as soon as you cross 40 years of age and if you are obese/overweight by 40 per cent you are prone to develop Diabetes. So keep your weight under control.
2. Regular Exercise and Balanced diet will keep your Diabetes under control.
3. Don't change the tablets which you are taking for the control of Diabetes on anybody's advice (except your doctor's) and don't take these tablets with alcohol.
4. Diabetics who smoke are the worst sufferers.
5. Don't substitute extra tablet for your extra food/ice cream.
6. Never stop your treatment by reading any advertisement in Newspaper for any magic medicine. You may disturb your well controlled disease by stopping treatment.
7. Avoid Sex therapies as all such treatment will not improve sexual performance until and unless your Diabetes is under control.
8. To improve the quality of life if you are advised Insulin treatment, it does not mean that your disease has reached at its end.
9. Don't stop your medication without doctor's advice.

Diabetes Care During Other Infections

When you get sick like have cold and cough, stomach upset, loose motions you may not be able to take your usual insulin or diabetes medicines as you normally take. You may not feel like eating. During this period blood sugar levels may go up or down.

What About Medicine Dosage

One should never stop taking medicine during this period. You may need extra dosage to control infection during certain infections when you are not able to take oral medicine. Your doctor would like to put you on regular insulins. This may be for limited period but essential to control infection.

If blood sugar is high, infections also become difficult to control. We have to control both infection and blood sugar at the same time.

Cough syrups, and Decongestants increase blood sugar. Asprin, crocin, some antibiotics may lower your blood glucose levels.

How About Food

You can eat your normal diet, sometimes semi-solids like Khichri (Rice+dal). *Daliya* (OAT). But consume plenty of liquids. If you have diarrhoea then take cup of fluid each hour.

You can use sugar free tea, coffee, lemon + salt in water. You can have fruit juices which have 15gm carbohydrate.

Blood Sugar Testing

Because of infections, and release of more hormones during this time, sugar levels fluctuates it is better to check your blood sugar level more often. Urine examination for ketones will help to rule out very high level of sugar.

Contact your Doctor

* If you are sick for more than 3-4 days.
* If you are having vomiting and loose motions.
* If blood sugar is above 250 mg/dl.
* If urine is showing ketones.
* If you have chest pain, breathing difficulty, fruity breath and dry tongue.

Timely help from doctor can help you to recover early.

Insulin Pumps

Insulin Pump is newer method of delivery of insulin in body by battery powered computerized device. Its size is about the size of mobile phone. Inside the pump is syringe which have short acting insulin with a gear driven plunger. A tube is attached to the pump and other end is attached with the needle or catheter which is inserted in the skin of abdomen or thigh and insulin is delivered through this into body.

Benefits

* Blood Glucose levels remain near normal
* If you have extreme fluctuations this will help you to smooth them out.
* You can adjust dose as per requirement of body.

Problems

* Biggest problem is cost of pump.
* *Infection* : Place where your body enters become infected always clean the area before you insert the needle by proper antibiotic lotion or cream.
* *Ketoacidosis*: Sometimes tube can get blocked then sugar levels may go high and person can develop diabetic ketoacidosis. Best way to protect is do frequent blood sugar monitoring.

Stress and Diabetes

Our lives are full of factors that can cause stress. Stress can be physical or stress can be mental, like job related marriage, etc. Good or bad stress which lasts longer affects your body. Diabetes is a physical stress. That lasts a long time.

During stress, hormones are pumped into your blood which in turn release stored blood glucose and stored fat for extra energy. This extra energy helps to face this stress.

In diabetic patients as there is not enough insulin, glucose and fat levels increase in the blood and this can lead to high blood sugar levels and high ketones.

Physical stress causes blood glucose levels to go up in most people with diabetes. Mental stress can influence in both ways—may cause blood sugar levels to go up and in some may lower blood sugar.

How to Handle Stress

1. Make lists of things that stress you.
2. Learn how you react to stress. You may feel tense, anxious, upset, or angry. You may feel tired, sad, or empty. You may have stomach up set or headache.
3. Change your reaction you can't stop things that cause stress. But you can change how you react. If you feel stressed try following tactics.

1. *Breathe Deeply*. This is called as *Sudershan kirya* too. You sit or lie down. Close your eyes. Breathe in deeply and slowly, breathe out slowly. Breathe in and out again (for 15 to 20 times). Start to relax your muscles. Do it twice in a day.

* Lie Down : Lie down close your eyes tense and relax the muscles of each part or body from head to feet.
* Loosen up and shake parts of body.
* Get a massage.
* Think about good things and talk about your troubles with family members or friends. Put your problems on paper.
* Stay active and listen to music you will find it soothing.
* Say no if you don't like anything.
* Have a hearty healthy laugh.
* Eat Wisely. During stress you may need more vitamins, protein and minerals. Eat, fruits like oranges, nuts, seeds, and beans, chicken, fish and egg white.
  For minerals :- low fat milk, curd and cheese.
* Get 6-8 hours of sleep a day.

Diet During Illness

If you feel ill or are unable to have your usual meals, it is important to:

1. Have your usual dose of Insulin or tablets at your normal time.
2. If you are too sick to eat your usual diet, you must substitute suitable food or fluids for the carbohydrate exchanges in your diet.
   Try some of the alternatives given below.
   Each one of the following is approximately 1 Carbohydrate Exchange

150-200ml	Fruit juice
150 ml	Ordinary lemonade/ordinary soft drink
1/2 cup	Ordinary Jelly
2 or 3	Dry biscuits
2 scoops	Ice cream

3. If you are vomiting or have diarrhoea, the risk of hypoglycaemia and dehydration will be greatly reduced if you take small amounts of sugar containing fluids every 30 minutes, e.g. 1/2 cup of ordinary lemonade.
   Plenty of additional fluid is also advisable.
   If your Blood Sugar Levels are persistently above 270 mg% take clear fluids (e.g. clear broths, water, diet soft drinks and diet coke).
4. Test your Blood Sugar level more frequently, perhaps every hour, and test your urine for ketone.

Remember :

* Take your usual Insulin or tablets
* Test Blood Sugar Levels more frequently
* Test for ketones
* Call your doctor

Foods Can be Used Freely

The following foods may be used freely to increase the variety in your meals.

Vegetables	—	All vegetables except potato, corn and legumes.
Fruits	—	lemon lime, Malta/Grape fruit, small quantities of watermelon, Guava and berries. One apple or two oranges or two slices of Papaya or Guava or combination of above in small amount can be taken.
Beverages	—	Tea, coffee, soda and plain mineral water, clear soups/broth.
Miscellaneous	—	Herbs and spices, garlic, ginger, mustard, chilli powder, curry paste and powder, vinegar, no oil dressings, tomato paste, tomato puree, essences such as vanilla, lemon and peppermint, cocoa.
Use Sparingly (as high in salt)	—	Meat and fish pastes.

Acceptable Special Diet Foods

— Artificial sweetners (liquid, powder, tablets)
Aspartame (Nutrasweet)
Saccharine, Cyclamate
Acesulphame K, Sucralose (Splenda)
Isomalt, maltodextrin, polydextrose

— **Products**
diet jellies
diet soft drinks
Diet topping
Sugarless chewing gum

Note: During pregnancy, Aspartame or Acesulphame K in small amounts are the preferred artificial sweetners.

Diet Charts

These Diet Charts are according to food habits of different regions of India—North India or South India

Diet Chart for Over Weight and Obese (Fat) Persons

1200 Calories

Sample Menu

	North	*South*	*East*	*West*
Pre-breakfast				
	1tea without Sugar 4 Marie biscuits 1/2 apple orange	1 coffee without sugar 3 banana chips biscuits 1/2 apple	1tea without sugar 4 Marie biscuits 1/2 small	1 coffee or tea without sugar 4 Marie biscuits 1/2 apple
Breakfast				
	2 slices bread	2 Idlies with chutney	2 slices bread	2 slices bread
	1 glass skimmed milk 1 egg	1 glass skimmed milk 1 egg	1 glass skimmed milk 1 egg	1 glass skimmed milk 1 egg
Lunch				
	3 Chapaties	2 katories rice	2 Katories rice	1 1/2 chapaties and 1 katorie rice
	1/2 Katori vegetable I teaspoon oil for cooking 2/3 glass curd	1/4 Katori sambar 1 teaspoon oil for cooking 2/3 glass curd	1/2 Katori vegetable 1 teaspoon oil for cooking 2/3 glass curd	1/2 Katori vegetable 1 teaspoon oil for cooking 2/3 glass curd
Evening snack				
	1 tea without sugar 2 Monaco biscuits 1/2 apple	1 coffee without sugar 2 Monaco biscuits 1/2 orange	1 tea without sugar 2 Monaco biscuits 1 piece papaya	1 coffee or tea without sugar 2 Monaco biscuits 1/2 apple

Dinner				
	2 Chapaties	1 Katori rice+ 1 1/2 chapaties	2 katories rice and 1 katori rice	1 1/2 chapaties
	1 Katori vegetable	1 Katori sambar	1 katori vegetable	1 Katori vegetable
	1 teaspoon oil for cooking	1 teaspoon oil for cooking	1teaspoon oil for cooking	1 teaspoon oil for cooking
	1/3 glass curd	1/3 glass curd	1/3 glass curd	1/3glass curd
	1/2 katori Rajmah	1/2 katori lentils	1/2 katori lentils	1/2 katori lentiles

Diet Chart for Overweight and Obese Persons

1400 calories

Sample Menu

	North	*South*	*East*	*West*
Pre-breakfast				
	1tea without sugar	1 coffee without sugar	1 tea without sugar	1 coffee or tea without sugar
	4 Marie biscuits	3 banana chips biscuits	4 Marie biscuits	4 Marie biscuits
	1/2 apple or orange	1/2 apple	1/2 small orance	1/2 apple
Breakfast				
	3 slices bread	3Idlies with chutney	3 slices bread	3 slices bread
	1 teaspoon butter	1 teaspoon oil for cooking	1 teaspoon oil for cooking	1 teaspoon oil for cooking
	1 glass skimmed milk	1 glass skimmed milk	1 glass skimmed milk	1 glass skimmed milk
	1 egg	1 egg	1 egg	1 egg
Lunch				
	3 Chapaties	2 katories rice	2 Katories rice	1 1/2 chapaties and 1 katori rice
	1/2 Katori vegetable	1/2 katori sambar	1katori vegetable	1 Katori vegetable
	1 teaspoon oil for cooking	1 teaspoon oil for cooking	1 teaspoon oil for cooking	1 teaspoon oil for cooking
	1/3 glass curd	1/3 glass curd	1/3 glass curd	1/3 glass curd
	1/2 Katori Rajmah	1/2 kator Lentils	1/2 Katori Lentils	1/2 Katori Lentils

Evening snack				
	1 tea without sugar 2 Monaco biscuits 1/2 apple	1 coffee without sugar 2 Monaco biscuits 1/2 orange	1 tea without sugar 2 Monaco biscuits 1 piece papaya	1 coffee or tea without sugar 2Monaco biscuits 1/2 apple
Dinner				
	2 Chapaties	1 Katori rice+ 1-1/2 chapaties	2 katories rice	1-1/2 chapaties and 1 katori rice
	1/2 Katori vegetable	1/2 Katori sambar	1/2 katori vegetable	1/2 Katori vegetable
	2/3glass curd	1/3glass curd	1/3glass curd	1/3glass curd
	1 teaspoon oil for cooking	1 teaspoon oil for cooking	1teaspoon oil for cooking	1 teaspoon oil for cooking
	1 piece chicken breast	1 piece chicken breast	1 piece fish	1 piece chicken breast

Diet Chart for Persons Working in Office, Doctors, Business Food Chart according to different regions of India

1800 calories

Sample Menu

	North	*South*	*East*	*West*
Pre-breakfast				
	1tea without Sugar 4 Monaco biscuits 1/2 apple	1 coffee without sugar 6 banana chips biscuits 1/2 small apple	1tea without sugar 4 Monaco biscuits 1/2 small orange	1 coffee or tea without sugar 4 Monaco biscuits 1/2 apple
Breakfast				
	4 slice bread	4 Idlies with chutney	4 slices bread	4 slices bread
	1teaspoon butter	1 teaspoon oil for cooking	1 teaspoon oil for cooking	1 teaspoon butter for cooking
	1 glass skimmed milk	1 glass skimmed milk	1 glass skimmed milk	1 glass skimmed milk
	1 egg	1 egg	1 egg	1 egg

Lunch				
	3 Chapaties	2 katories rice	2 Katories rice	1-1/2 chapaties and 1 katori rice
	1 Katori vegetable	1/2 katori sambar	1 katorie vegetable	1 Katorie vegetable
	1-1/2 teaspoon oil for cooking	1-1/2 teaspoon oil for cooking	1-1/2 teaspoon oil for cooking	1-1/2teaspoon oil for cooking
	2/3 glass curd	2/3 glass curd	2/3 glass curd	2/3 glass curd
	3/4 Katori Rajmah	3/4 katori Lentils	3/4 Katori Lentils	3/4 Katori Lentils
Evening snack				
	1 tea without sugar	1 coffee without sugar	1 tea without sugar	1 coffee or tea without sugar
	8 Maire biscuits	8 Maire biscuits	8 Maire biscuits	8 Maire biscuits
	1/2 apple	1/2 orange	2 piece papaya	1/2 apple
Dinner				
	3 Chapaties+1 katori rice	2Katories rice+ 1-1/2 chapaties	3katories rice &2 chapaties	1-1/2 chapaties
	1Katori vegetable	1Katori vegetable	1katori vegetable	1Katori vegetable
	1-1/2 teaspoon oil for cooking	1-1/2 teaspoon oil for cooking	1-1/2 teaspoon oil for cooking	1-1/2 teaspoon oil for cooking
	1/3 glass curd	1/3 glass curd	1/3 glass curd	1/3 glass curd
	1 piece chicken	1 piece chicken	1 piece fish	1 piece chicken

The vegetables may be used as desired. Carbohydrates and calories are negligible.

Leafy Vegetables		*Other vegetables*	
Bitter gourd (karela)	Curry leaves	Brinjal	Onion stalks
Amarnath	Fenugreek leaves	Cauliflower	Pumpkin
Bathua	Lettuce	Cucumber	Radish
Brussels sprouts	Mint	Drumstick	Tinda
Cabbage	Spinach	French beans	Tomato, Green
Celery	Soya Leaves	Ladies Finger	Turnip
Coriander leaves		Mango, green	

For Persons Who do Strenuous Job (Hard Work)

2000 calories

SAMPLE MENU

	North	*South*	*East*	*West*
Pre-breakfast				
	1tea without Sugar	1 coffee without sugar	1tea without sugar	1 coffee or tea without sugar
	4 Marie and 2 Monaco biscuits	6 banana chips 2 Monaco biscuits	4 Marie and 2 Monaco biscuits	4 Marie and 2 Monaco biscuits
	1/2 apple	1/2 small apple	1small orange	1 apple
Breakfast				
	4 slice bread	4 Idlies with chutney	4 slices bread	4 slices bread
	1teaspoon butter	1 teaspoon oil for cooking	1 teaspoon butter	1 teaspoon butter
	1 glass skimmed milk	1 glass skimmed milk	1 glass skimmed milk	1 glass skimmed milk
	2 eggs	2 eggs	2 eggs	2 eggs
Lunch				
	4-1/2 Chapaties	3 katories rice	3 Katories rice	1-1/2 chapaties and 2 katories rice
	1 Katori vegetable	1/2 katori sambar	1 katori vegetable	1 Katori vegetable
	2 teaspoon oil for cooking	2 teaspoon oil for cooking	2 teaspoon oil for cooking	2 teaspoon oil for cooking
	2/3 glass curd	2/3 glass curd	2/3 glass curd	2/3 glass curd
	3/4 Katori Rajmah	3/4 katori Lentils	3/4 Katori Lentils	3/4 Katori Lentils
Evening snack				
	1 tea without sugar	1 coffee without sugar	1 tea without sugar	1 coffee or tea without sugar
	4 Maire and 2 Monaco biscuits	4 Maire and 2 Monaco biscuits	4 Maire and 2 Monaco biscuits	4 Maire and 2 Monaco biscuits
	1/2 apple	1/2 apple	2 piece orange	1/2 apple

Dinner

3 Chapaties+	2 Katories rice+	3 katories rice	11/2chapaties
1 katori rice	1-1/2 chapaties		& 2 chapaties
1Katori vegetable	1Katori vegetable	1katori vegetable	1Katori vegetable
1-1/2 teaspoon oil for cooking	1-1/2 teaspoon oil for cooking	1-1/2 teaspoon oil for cooking	1-1/2 teaspoon oil for cooking
1/3 glass curd	1/3 glass curd	1/3 glass curd	1/3 glass curd
1 piece chicken	1 piece chicken	1 piece fish	1 piece chicken

Food Values and General Guidelines.

Desserts*

	Household Measures	*Wt/Vol*	*Calories*
Custard		150gm	360
Fruits salad		150gm	150
Fruits Salad with cream		150gm	300
Ice, Cream		150 gm	380
Carrot halwa	1 medium katori	100 gm	600
Badami Halwa		100gm	570

Sweets*

	Household Measures	*Wt/Vol*	*Calories*
Coconut burfi		25gm	110
Gulab jamun		25gm	200
Ladoo		30gm	160
Rasgula		150 gm	140
Jam	2 table spoon		80
Honey	3 table spoon		48

Beverages**

Beer	150ml	65
Wine dry	30ml	30
Wine dessert	30ml	40
Whisky, brandy, gin, rum	30ml	65
Vodka	30 ml	65
Ginger etc.	30 ml	9

* It is better to avoid alcohol. Too much alcohol may cause low blood sugar by potentiating the effect of insulin or drugs and blocking glucose production in the liver while adding to calories. It can cause increase in cholesterol and triglycerides.

* Artificial sweetners like Aspartame and saccharine tables are available. They are safe and may be used in moderate amounts.
* Vegetables mentioned under the List 8 vegetable exchange have negligible calories and may be used whenever desirable.
* Avoid or restrict foodstuffs high in saturated fat and cholesterol.
* Avoid sweet foods, jams, chocolates, cakes, sweet cream, which increase triglyceride levels.
* Bake, roast, boil or steam instead of frying food.
* Do not replace oil and fat with calories in terms of sweets which when taken in excess gets converted to triglycerides.

Calorie Count/Content in Food

The nutritional unit of energy is calorie for the body. If foodstuffs are not replaced in equal amount, the body becomes thinner the quantity of calories per item are given below.

These are average figures, because the food values of raw materials can vary considerably.

Beverages

Beverages	*Approximate Measures/Weight*	*Caloric Content (K Cal)*
Aerated soft drinks	1 bottle	78
Lemonade	1 glass (250 ml.)	90
Fruit juices		
Apple	3/4 glass	87
Sweet Lime (fresh)	1glass	52
Orange (fresh)	1 glass	111
Pineapple (canned)	3/4 glass	104

Beverages	*Approximate Measures/Weight*	*Caloric Content (K Cal)*
Tomato (canned)	3/4 glass	34
Coconut water	1 coconut	120
Tea (clear, unsweetened)	1 cup (125ml.)	2
Coffee (clear, unsweetened)	1 cup	5
Chocolate (all milk)	1 glass	208
Bournvita powder	3 teaspoon full	88
Horlicks	5 teaspoon full	88
Protinex	2 teaspoon full	88
Soups		
Clear vegetable soup	1 cup	negligible
Chicken noodles soup	1 cup	59
Chicken soup	1 cup	75
Cream of tomato	1 cup	173
Cream of mushroom	1 cup	149
Cream of peas	1 cup	128
Alcoholic Beverages		
Beer	1 glass	114
Rum	1 jigger (45ml.)	105
Gin	I jigger (45ml.)	105
Whisky	1 jigger (45ml.)	105
Champagne	1 glass	84
Sherry	1 glass	84
Vodka	1 jigger (45ml.)	125

Cooked Food

Food	*Approx. weight*	*Approx. Calories (K Cal)*
Plain Dosa	100 gms.	360
Iddli	100 gms.	132
Pongal	100 gms.	356

Food	*Approx. weight*	*Approx. Calories (K Cal)*
Uthappam	100 gms.	330
Puri	40 gms.	184
Khichadi	100 gms.	168
Papdi Chat	100 gms.	474
Dhokla	100 gms.	122
Uppama	100 gms.	233
Poha	100 gms.	118
Muruku	100 gms.	529
Namkeen	100 gms.	521
Mathi	100 gms.	521
Samosa	100 gms.	256
Khakra	40 gms.	140
Adai	100 gms.	571
Aapam	100 gms.	226
Chiwda	100 gms.	420
Potato chips	20 gms.	113
Cheese Pizza	60 gms.	145
Ham Burger	90 gms.	244
Cheese Burger	100 gms.	290

Food	*Calories/100gms. (K.cal.)*
Bread	
Wholemeal	224
Granary white and brown	245-225.5
Cheese	
Cottage (low-fat)	105-115.5
Cream	445
Chutney	70-140

	Calories/100gms. (K.cal.)
Fats and oils	
Butter, margarine	738.5
Oils	892.5
Outline low fat spread	367.5
Fresh Fruits	
Apples, grapes, cherries	49
Soft fruit	21
Grapefruit	21
Melon	21
Orange, peaches	35
Pears, pineapples, plums	42
Fruit canned	77-105 (average)
Honey	287-315
Ice-cream	175
Jams	280 (average)
Fresh Meat	
Chicken	108.5
Liver	133
Pork	189
Milk	
Whole liquid	63
Dried skimmed	325.5
Soya liquid	35
Nuts, Shelled	
Cashew	623
Coconut	343
Hazel	378
Peanuts	581
Walnuts	528.5
Peanut	630
Fresh vegetable	
Lettuce, mushroom celery	7
Turnips	14

	Calories/100gms. (K.cal.)
Carrots, onions	21
Cauliflower, spring greens	25
Peas	63
Potatoes	84
Sweet peas, sweet corn	98
Wheat germ	350
Fruit-flavoured	77(average)

Calorie Consumption

Calorie Consumption	*Body weight kgs.*			
Per hour on the job	*58*	*65*	*75*	*85*
Driving (active)	204	228	252	276
Keyboarding	126	138	150	162
Managerial (desk sedentary)	204	228	252	276
Managerial (active)	222	246	270	294
Telephone Conversation	198	222	246	270
Teaching	204	228	252	276
Writing (sitting)	102	120	132	150
Exercising Badminton singles	312	348	384	420
Doubles	270	306	342	378
Dancing				
Aerobic (medium)	396	444	492	540
Contemporary (rock)	228	258	252	318
Golf				
Driving	228	258	228	318
Putting	138	156	174	192
Hill climbing	534	600	666	732
Running				
9 km/hr.	594	660	732	804
11 km/hr.	624	696	768	840
12 km/hr.	672	816	960	1104

Calorie Consumption	*Body weight kgs.*			
Per hour on the job	*58*	*65*	*75*	*85*
Swimming				
Slow	270	306	242	588
Medium	480	534	594	642
Fast	618	696	342	378
Tennis				
Singles	378	420	462	510
Doubles	270	306	342	378
Walking				
3.2 km./hr.	168	192	216	240
4.8 km./hr.	270	306	342	378
6.4 km.hr.	312	354	396	438
8 km./hr.	204	228	252	276
Yoga	204	228	252	276
Others				
Cooking	165	192	216	240
Card playing	90	102	114	132
Eating	84	90	96	102
Showering and dressing	180	204	228	252
Sitting quietly	72	84	96	108
Sitting talking	90	102	114	132
Sleeping	60	66	72	78
Waiting in line	90	102	114	132
Watching TV	78	90	96	102

Fruits to be avoided

Banana, Mango, Cheeku, Grapes, Sharifa should be avoided as they contain plenty of calories and sugar.

2. Cooking Oils

All cooking oils have same fat and calorie content but some may contain more fatty acids while other less.

Oils (fats) containing more saturated fatty acids should be avoided like *Vanaspati, coconut oil* and *margarine* should be avoided. While Ghee and butter may be used cautiously.

Oils which can be safely used.

Sunflower oil	Groundnut oil
Sunflower oil	Sesame oil
Corn oil	Soyabean oil

Foods to be avoided

Sugar and Gud
Jam, Candies
Chocobar
Sweet, Achar-Pickles
Sonth
Beer, Whisky, Sherbat
Pineapple juice (tinned)
Cold drinks
Boost, Maltova, Horlicks, Bournvita

Fruits permitted

Citrus fruits like Orange, Malta, Mosamabi, Kinnu, Grape fruit, Apple, Watermelon and Papaya can be taken. One can have one or two of the above fruits or above 100-150 gm. In case of watermelon one can have 400 gm as it contains plenty of water.

Height and Weight Table

Height (cm), Weight (kg.)— for Indian Males

Height (cm)	*Age in years* 20 kg	25 kg	30 kg	35 kg	40 kg	45 kg	50 kg
148	42.7	44.2	46.2	47.6	48.8	50.0	50.9
150	43.6	44.9	46.9	48.5	49.7	50.8	51.5
153	45.5	47.0	49.0	50.4	51.7	52.3	53.5
155	46.3	48.1	49.9	51.5	52.7	53.5	54.2
158	48.9	50.0	52.0	53.5	54.5	55.7	56.6
160	49.7	51.1	53.1	54.7	55.6	56.7	57.4
163	51.1	52.7	54.9	56.3	57.6	58.5	59.4
165	53.1	54.7	56.9	58.5	59.6	60.6	62.0
168	54.0	56.3	58.1	60.1	61.5	62.4	53.7
170	56.5	57.9	60.3	62.2	63.7	64.7	65.8
173	58.1	60.1	62.2	64.0	65.8	67.0	68.3
175	60.1	62.2	64.2	66.0	68.1	68.7	71.0
178	61.9	64.0	66.3	68.5	70.6	71.9	72.4
180	64.0	66.2	68.5	71.0	73.3	74.4	75.1
183	66.0	68.5	71.0	73.3	75.6	77.1	77.8
148	38.6	41.0	42.6	44.0	45.1	46.3	47.1
150	40.3	41.6	43.5	44.8	46.0	47.0	47.7
153	41.9	43.5	45.3	46.6	47.9	48.4	49.5
155	42.8	44.3	46.2	47.7	48.8	49.5	50.1
158	44.9	46.3	48.1	49.5	50.5	51.6	52.1
160	46.0	47.3	49.1	50.6	51.5	52.4	53.0
163	47.3	48.8	50.8	52.1	52.2	54.1	54.9
165	49.1	50.6	52.6	54.1	55.3	56.0	57.3
148	42.7	44.2	46.2	47.6	48.8	50.0	50.9
148	38.6	41.0	42.6	44.0	45.1	46.3	47.1
150	40.3	41.3	43.5	44.8	46.0	47.0	47.7
153	41.9	43.5	45.3	46.6	47.9	48.4	49.5
155	42.8	44.3	46.2	47.7	48.8	49.5	50.1
158	44.9	46.3	48.1	49.5	50.5	51.6	52.1
160	46.0	47.3	49.1	50.6	51.5	52.4	53.0
163	47.3	48.8	50.8	52.1	52.2	54.1	54.9

Calories Values

Breakfast Food

Foodstuff	*Calories*	*Fat Saturated (gm)*	*Total (gm)*	*Cholesterol (mg)*
Bacon Fried 1 slice (25gms)	95	2.8	9.0	3.0
Bread, White 2 Slice (40 gms)	98	-	0.3	-
Bun 1 big (60 gms)	170	-	0.4	-
Cheese Toast 2 Slice (70 gms)	220	8.0	13.1	19.5
Corn Flakes 1 cup without milk & sugar	95	-	Traces	-
Dosa—Masala/Mysore With butter (200 gms)	400	9.0	25.0	42.0
Dosa, Plain (50 gms)	200	7.0	10.0	-
Egg, White 1 white (17gms)	15	-	-	-
Egg Whole (50 gms)	87	1.7	6.6	248.0
Egg, Yolk 1 yolk (33gms)	62	1.7	6.6	248.0
Egg, Boiled (50 gms)	87	1.7	6.6	248.0
Egg (fried/omelet/scrambled)				
(a) suing 1 tbsp. (15 gm) butter/ghee	200	16.1	18.7	290.0
(b) using 1 tbsp Oil	225	11.2	21.6	248.0
Finger Chips 1 serving	465	21.0	30.2	-

Foodstuff	*Calories*	*Fat Saturated (gm)*	*Total (gm)*	*Cholesterol (mg)*
Fruit Bread 1 slice (20gms)	60	0.1	1.0	-
Ham, Roasted 1 slice (50 gms)	245	10.4	25.0	25.0
Idli with sambar (60gms)	250	1.0	5.0	-
Luncheon Meat 1 slice (20gms)	65	1.7	5.0	3.0
Milk bread 1 slice (20gms)	55	0.1	5.0	0.2
Milk, skimmed 1 cup (200ml)	74	-	0.2	0.4
Milk, whole 1 cup (200ml)	150	4.9	8.1	22.0
Parotha, Plain (50gms)	250	7.0	12.5	28.0
Parotha, stuffed (70gms)	300	7.0	12.5	28.0
Sausages, Cooked (25gms)	85	1.6	7.0	25.0
Salami 1 slice (10gms)	45	3.1	7.0	-
Tomato Omelet (60gms)	250	7.0	12.0	-
Uthappam, Onion (75gms)	275	7.0	10.8	-
Uppama 1 plate (150gms)	235	3.5	8.0	-
SNACKS 'N' SAVOURIES				
Belpuri 1 plate (150gms)	185	3.5	5.5	-
Biscuits, salted (10gms)	53	0.3	3.2	-

Foodstuff	*Calories*	*Fat Saturated (gm)*	*Total (gm)*	*Cholesterol (mg)*
Biscuits, Sweet (10gms)	45	0.1	1.3	-
Cutlets, Mutton (200gms)	480	18.5	28.5	95.0
Cutlets, Vegetable (200gms)	450	17.5	25.0	-
Dahi-Vada (200 gms)	250	10.5	19.5	-
Dalwada (60 gms)	340	9.0	15.0	-
Farsan/Chewada 1 plate (100gms)	230	10.5	15.0	-
Kachoris (150gms)	400	14.0	20.0	-
Patties (200gms)	300	7.0	10.0	-
Paneer Pakoda (50gms)	275	15.2	22.0	20.0
Pizza (Meat) 1 small (225gms)	400	14.5	20.0	75.0
Pizza (Vegetable, Cheese) 1 small (200gms)	325	11.7	15.0	32.5
Potato Wadas (150gms)	470	14.0	20.0	-
Puri Bhaji 1 plate (250gms)	685	27.0	42.0	-
Ragada Patties 1 plate (250gms)	450	7.0	13.0	-
Samosa (150gms)	500	14.0	20.0	-
Sev Puri 1 plate (200gms)	225	10.5	15.0	-
Bhajias, Onion 1 plate (150gms)	395	17.5	27.6	-
Cauliflower Pakoras 1 plate (150gms)	410	17.5	27.9	-

Foodstuff	*Calories*	*Fat Saturated (gm)*	*Total (gm)*	*Cholesterol (mg)*
Almonds (100gms)	655	4.2	58.9	-
Cashewnuts (100gms)	596	9.3	46.9	-
Pistachios (100gms)	680	7.8	57.8	-
Walnuts (100gms)	687	6.6	64.5	-
MEALS				
a. Soups				
Chicken Soup 1 cup	185	6.8	12.5	87.0
Chicken Vegetable Soup 1 cup	162	4.4	8.7	73.0
Corn Soup (Sweet) 1 cup	120	1.7	7.0	248.0
Dal Soup 1 cup	137	2.2	4.2	14.0
Green Peas Soup 1 cup	176	2.2	5.5	14.0
Spinach Soup 1 cup	50	2.2	4.4	14.0
Tomato Soup 1 cup	87	2.2	4.2	14.0
Each cup equivalent to 200ml				
b. Salads				
Russian Salad 1 serving (100gm)	545	18.1	50.0	289
Sprouted Pulse Salad 1 serving (100gm)	225	3.5	5.7	-
c. Vegetable				
Brinjal Bhartah 1 serving (150gm)	150	7.0	10.5	-
Chana Masala 1 serving (200gm)	240	7.0	10.0	-

Foodstuff	*Calories*	*Fat Saturated (gm)*	*Total (gm)*	*Cholesterol (mg)*
Chana Dal 1 bow/1 cup (150gms)	270	7.0	17.8	-
Dum Aloo 1 serving (150gm)	254	10.8	15.7	1.6
Macaroni & Tomato (butter) 1 serving (150gms)	396	15.4	27.3	70
Mixed Vegetables— Carrots Peas, Cauliflower, Beans etc. 1 serving (150gm)	175	7.0	10.5	-
Palak Paneer 1 serving (150gm)	180	11.0	13.0	20.0
Potato & Peas 1 serving (150gm)	235	7.0	10.0	-
Paneer Tikka 1 serving (150gm)	285	16.4	25.0	42.3
Potato Vegetable 1 serving (150gm)	165	7.0	11.2	-
MEALS				
Dal Bhaji (Spinach & Bengal Gram Dal) 1 serving (150gm)	125	3.5	7.0	-
Stuffed Bhindi 1 serving (150gm)	200	3.5	6.2	-
Stuffed Capsicum (Simla Mirch) 1 serving (150gm)	120	3.5	6.0	-
Stuffed Karela 1 serving (150gm)	275	17.5	28.5	-
Vegetables, Leafy 1 serving (100gm)	100	3.5	5.5	-
Vegetables, Baked 1 serving (150gm)	395	6.7	22.5	5.3

Foodstuff	*Calories*	*Fat Saturated (gm)*	*Total (gm)*	*Cholesterol (mg)*
d. Cereals				
Bhakri (Jowar, Bajra, Ragi) 1 med. (90gms)	300	-	1.5	-
Biryani Mutton 1 med. Bowl (150gms)	255	11.5	16.5	-
Chappati 1 med. (30 gms)	100	-	0.5	-
Chappati with ghee 1 tsp 1 med. (30 gms)	150	2.3	5.5	-
Fried Rice 1 med. Bowl (150 gms)	20	5.2	7.5	-
Khichadi 1 serving (150 gms)	190	3.5	10.0	-
Naan 1 no. (20gms)	225	2.1	3.4	-
Puris 1 no. (20 gms)	105	4.2	6.2	-
Pulao, Vegetable 1 med. Bowl (100gms)	170	3.5	5.0	-
Rice cooked 1 med. Bowl (100gms)	100	-	-	-
Khadi 1 bow/cup (200ml)	150	7.5	11.0	2.7
Kofta Curry 1 serving (200ml)	225	10.0	15.0	-
Lauki Dal 1 bowl/cup (200ml)	150	7.0	11.5	-
Rajma Curry 1 bowl/cup (200ml)	290	7.0	10.7	-
Prawn Pulao 1 serving	510	7.3	32.5	150
Egg Fried Rice 1 serving	280	1.7	16.7	248

Foodstuff	Calories	Fat Saturated (gm)	Total (gm)	Cholesterol (mg)
NON-VEGETARIAN				
Chicken Butter 1 serving	305	11.4	21.0	160
Chicken Curry 1 serving	175	7.1	10.4	70
Chicken Chilli 1 serving	255	10.5	16.0	90
Chicken Fried in Butter 1 serving	440	15.0	25.5	217
Chicken Paella 1 serving	325	10.5	15.8	45
Chicken Patties 2 pieces	335	14.0	20.4	45
Chopsuey 1 serving	150	7.3	11.4	18
Egg Curry 1 serving	235	12.4	21.5	248
Elaichi Mutton 1 serving	215	1.5	13.6	70
Fish Baked 1 serving	395	8.7	32.3	107
Fish Curry 1 serving	35	3.5	7.0	50
Fish & Chips 1 serving	850	35.2	52.8	130
Fish in Curds (Hilsa) 1 serving	505	14.5.	40.5	82
Fish Fried 1 piece (50 gms)	220	10.5	17.5	50
Kheema Mutton 1 serving	240	8.5	13.6	70
Mutton Curry 1 serving	185	8.0	12.7	95

Foodstuff	*Calories*	*Fat Saturated (gm)*	*Total (gm)*	*Cholesterol (mg)*
Mutton Vindaloo 1 serving	334	18.5	28.6	70
Nargisi Kabab 2 pieces	360	17.0	29.3	301
Pork Curry 1 serving	185	8.3	13.5	80
Pork Sorpote (Goan) 1 serving	321	15.4	25.1	165
Prawns Fried 1 serving	273	14.1	21.0	150
Prawn Malaya Curry 1 serving	415	28.0	32.4	150
Stewed Mutton 1 serving	145	4.5	7.5	95
Stuffed Mutton Malai Kofta 1 serving	600	27.0	50.0	215
Sweet & Sour Mutton 1 serving	285	10.5	20.5	176

Note: Each serving equivalent to 150 gms unless indicated otherwise.

ORGAN MEAT				
Brain (100gms)	107	2.4	8.5	2235
Heart Goat (100gms)	115	1.5	5.0	256
Kidney Goat (100gms)	120	4.2	11.0	700
Liver				
Goat (100gms)	107	2.6	5.3	406
Lamb (100gms)	110	2.8	6.8	510
Pork (100gms)	110	2.9	5.5	420
SEA FOOD				
Crabs Cooked (75gms raw)	155	-	10.5	70

Foodstuff	Calories	Fat Saturated (gm)	Total (gm)	Cholesterol (mg)
Prawns, Cooked (75gms raw)	155	-	10.5	70
Lobsters (75gms raw)	165	-	12.0	70
SWEETS & DESSERTS				
Amriti (50gms)	295	10.5	16.0	-
Basundi 1 serving (150gms)	270	6.0	12.0	27.5
Besan Ladoo (50gms)	205	5.5	8.5	-
Bundi Ladoo (50gms)	210	5.2	8.5	-
Cake, Iced 1 slice (55 gms)	190	4.8	8.0	50.0
Cake, Plain 1 slice (40 gms)	118	1.0	2.5	30.0
Cake, Fruit 1 slice (40 gms)	155	3.6	6.2	30.0
Custard, Plain 1 serving (200gms)	220	5.0	8.2	22.0
Custard with Jelly 1 serving (225gms)	230	5.0	8.2	22.0
Fruit Salad 1 serving (225gms)	250	5.0	8.2	22.0
Gulab Jamun (60gms)	282	13.0	20.2	12.5
Halwa, Vegetable (carrot, pumpkin, gourd) 1 serving (200gms)	225	7.0	13.7	42.0
Ice-Cream (Small) 1 cup (100gms)	215	6.7	10.8	45.0
Jalebi (40gms)	280	10.5	16.0	-

Foodstuff	*Calories*	*Fat Saturated (gm)*	*Total (gm)*	*Cholesterol (mg)*
Kheer, Rice 1 avg. serving (200gms)	240	3.6	8.0	22.0
Kheer, Vermicelli 1 serving (200gms)	240	3.6	8.5	22.0
Modak, Fried (50 gms)	250	11.0	19.5	-
Modak Steamed (40gms)	160	5.2	9.4	-
Pudding, Bread 1 serving (150gms)	300	7.0	15.3	5.0
Pudding, Milk 1 serving (150gms)	280	7.0	14.8	58.0
Puran Poli (60gms)	315	14.0	26.0	-
Rasgulla (40gms)	180	2.4	4.2	7.0
Rewal Ladoo (50gms)	205	5.2	8.5	-
Rasmalai, 2 Rasgullas 1 serving (150gms)	370	9.6	12.5	29.0